ASSISTING STUDENTS WITH DISABILITIES

A Handbook for School Counselors

SECOND EDITION

Julie P. Baumberger • Ruth E. Harper

A JOINT PUBLICATION

AMERICAN
SCHOOL
COUNSELOR
ASSOCIATION

CORWIN PRESS
A SAGE Publications Company
Thousand Oaks, CA 91320

Corwin Press extends grateful acknowledgment to the American School Counselor Association (ASCA) for permission to reprint its position statement *The Professional School Counselor and Students With Special Needs* and its *Ethical Standards for School Counselors*.

For information:

Corwin Press
A Sage Publications Company
2455 Teller Road
Thousand Oaks, California 91320
www.corwinpress.com

Sage Publications Ltd.
1 Oliver's Yard
55 City Road
London EC1Y 1SP
United Kingdom

Sage Publications India Pvt. Ltd.
B–42, Panchsheel Enclave
Post Box 4109
New Delhi 110 017 India

Printed in the United States of America

Library of Congress Cataloging-in-Publication Data

Baumberger, Julie P.
Assisting students with disabilities: A handbook for school counselors / Julie
P. Baumberger and Ruth E. Harper. — 2nd ed.
    p. cm.
Includes bibliographical references and index.
ISBN 1-4129-4181-4 or 978-1-4129-4181-5 (cloth)
ISBN 1-4129-4182-2 or 978-1-4129-4182-2 (pbk.)
    1. Students with disabilities—Counseling of—United States. 2. Children with disabilities—Education—United States. 3. Educational counseling—United States. I. Harper, Ruth E. II. Title.
LC4031.B39 2007
371.91—dc22   2006020924

This book is printed on acid-free paper.

06   07   08   09   10   10   9   8   7   6   5   4   3   2   1

Acquisitions Editor:	Stacy Wagner
Editorial Assistant:	Joanna Coelho
Production Editor:	Melanie Birdsall
Copy Editor:	Thomas Burchfield
Typesetter:	C&M Digitals (P) Ltd.
Proofreader:	Gail Fay
Indexer:	Naomi Linzer
Cover Designer:	Scott Van Atta
Graphic Designer:	Lisa Riley

Contents

Foreword

As a counselor educator, I know the challenges of providing school counseling students with all the information they need to know as entering school counselors. One area that is often neglected is that of working with students who have disabilities. Given the increasing numbers of students with disabilities, as well as the changing and expanding roles of counselors with these students, an updated book on this topic is exactly what is needed. Dr. Baumberger and Dr. Harper have done an outstanding job of providing current and future school counselors with concrete, useful information they can use the same day they read the book.

This handbook is the perfect mix of practical application with the theoretical basis that helps the ideas make sense. The knowledge that counselors will gain by reading this book will definitely help them to become more effective and successful in working with the diverse population of students who receive special services. It is common and expected that school counselors are involved with *all* students, including those with special needs. Whatever role the counselors fulfill (e.g., direct services, observations, advocacy, etc.) or may take on, this book is a must read.

As a certified school counselor and licensed school psychologist, I found myself appreciating the clarity and direction that the authors provide—I was always eager to read the next chapter. I suspect that once you start reading and gaining a greater understanding of special education and the various roles of today's school counselors, you will have a very difficult time putting the book down. In fact, this is exactly the kind of book that we need more of in the profession. Soon you will enjoy the feeling of greater competence in working with students who have disabilities!

As you read and learn more about special education and the school counselor's role, I encourage you to share the information in this book with your colleagues. From student counselors to seasoned, school-based professionals, they will thank you for the referral and will find this book an invaluable tool.

—Jay Trenhaile, EdD
Department Head and Associate Professor
Counseling and Human Resource Development
South Dakota State University

Preface

This book is designed for school counselors who are looking to provide confident and competent guidance to students who have physical, emotional, and cognitive disabilities. It gives counselors a highly useful, easily referenced resource to keep close at hand. We are pleased to be publishing it now in its second edition, as the topic has even greater relevance today for school counselors, teachers, and parents of children with disabilities.

Since the first edition was published in 1999, the laws affecting people with disabilities have been reauthorized and strengthened, the No Child Left Behind (NCLB) Act was signed into law, and the incidence rate of a number of disabilities has increased. In response, many excellent Web sites and other new resources have emerged as strong assets for those working with and supporting students with disabilities. We have identified and recommended these new sources of information where relevant.

Readers of this edition will find additional elements that will assist school counselors in determining how best to serve students with disabilities. We have made every effort to include current information about the counseling needs of students with disabilities and how school counselors can best meet these needs. The information also has great relevance for teachers as well as parents of children with disabilities.

OVERVIEW OF CONTENTS

It is our sincere hope that this book will provide a good starting place for school counselors to proactively include all students in the delivery of a comprehensive guidance program. The thoroughly updated Chapter 1, covering special education law, describes the most recent changes shaping the legal context for working with this population of students. Knowledge of this context is important to school counselors as they work as members of school multidisciplinary teams.

Chapter 2 looks closely at specific learning disabilities, and the counselor's role in identifying them and developing counseling plans.

In Chapter 3, appropriate and timely assessment techniques are covered, and an updated and expanded case study is included that guides counselors through reporting assessment findings.

Chapter 4 helps readers connect data to appropriate interventions by exploring a comprehensive model we developed, known by the acronym TREAT: **T**heories and concepts, **R**elationships, **E**nvironment, **A**djunct services, and **T**reatable goals and objectives. This model provides goals that are helpful in designing effective interventions for students with disabilities. It also represents a focused approach that draws information and interpretation from all stakeholders (identified student, parents, teachers, counselors, and others). A worksheet for applying the TREAT model is included.

Chapter 5 discusses identifying, designing, and carrying out both measurable and manageable counseling goals for students with disabilities and provides examples of behavioral and affective goals. The chapter also provides a rationale for why school counselors must be involved in establishing any and all goals for which they will be responsible.

Chapter 6 covers working with families and encourages school counselors to adopt both a solution-focused and systems perspective—at least to some extent—when working with students and families. Examples of how to establish trust with parents, as well as how to consider the needs of the siblings of children who have disabilities, are included.

Chapter 7 challenges and encourages school counselors to provide leadership, advocacy, collaboration, and systemic change when meeting the needs of students with disabilities.

Professional school counselors can and do make a difference in the lives of the students they serve, but they are sometimes expected to do too much or to assume inappropriate roles. Reading this book and applying the knowledge gained from it will help counselors meet the growing challenges in their schools with a renewed sense of self-assurance and belief in what they do. In this way, school counselors can continue to demonstrate the value of their role and the contributions that the comprehensive school counseling program makes to students, families, schools, and society at large. A suggested reading list is included for readers who would like to explore certain topics in greater depth.

We appreciate having the opportunity to update this resource, and hope that this book is useful in meeting the goal of increasing effective counseling services for all students.

Acknowledgments

M any parents and school counselors lent their perspectives and wisdom to our work. In particular, we thank Hande Briddick, Catherine Crews, Gary Gibson, Julie Gnadt, Jill Kessler, Nadine Porter, and Larry Rogers for their interest and insight. A special message of gratitude is extended to Emily Levine and Jay Trenhaile, whose personal support and professional contributions have been significant throughout the project.

We want to acknowledge Stacy Wagner, our acquisitions editor, for providing us this opportunity to explore, think, and write on a topic we feel passionate about. We thank Melanie Birdsall for coordinating production so ably. And finally, "Ruth, what do we do about Bob?"

Corwin Press wishes to thank the following peer reviewers for their editorial insight and guidance:

Greg Conderman
Associate Professor of Special Education
Northern Illinois University
DeKalb, Illinois

Mary Lanham
Guidance Counselor
Orange Park Elementary School
Orange Park, Florida

LeAnn Pollard
School Counselor
Hogan-Spring Glen Elementary School
Jacksonville, Florida

About the Authors

Julie P. Baumberger is Associate Professor at the Ross School of Medicine (Dominica, West Indies), where she has a joint appointment in the Department of Behavioral Sciences and the Counseling Center. She also teaches for Capella University in the Harold Abel School of Psychology. As a licensed professional counselor, psychological examiner, and school counselor, Baumberger worked for many years as a school counselor in both elementary and secondary schools. She later maintained a private practice counseling children, youth, and adults. Her current research and scholarly interests include youth and adults with disabilities, school counselor preparation, and mental health issues of young adults pursuing medical education.

Ruth E. Harper is Professor of Counseling and Human Resource Development at South Dakota State University, where she coordinates the college student personnel track. Harper has been a counselor and administrator at the postsecondary level for many years. Harper's research and writing focuses on college student mental health issues, American Indian college students, and career counseling.

This book is dedicated to our children,
Laura and Jay, Adam, Jennie, and Jordan,
and to
Libby, Betsy, and Maggie,
who taught us that there are many ways to learn.

CHAPTER ONE

The Legal Context for Working With Students With Disabilities

I t is the end of another busy school day. As you walk to the main office, you mentally check off the elements of your day's to-do list. You have met with teachers, conducted classroom guidance, and led small groups on changes in family systems. You worked on a curriculum for conflict resolution in the classroom and made several telephone contacts with parents. It has turned out to be a productive day with few interruptions. As you enter the main office to pick up your messages and a final cup of coffee before heading home, you see something in your box that always makes you apprehensive: an invitation to an Individualized Education Program (IEP) meeting. You care deeply about the success of all students in your school, and you are a committed team player, but these meetings remind you that you have very little training in working with students with special needs.

Each time you attend an IEP meeting, the requests for your time and skills are different. Last week's student has low self-esteem, seems disinterested in school, will not finish his work, and rejects authority figures. You are expected to take the lead on these issues, collaborating with special and general education teachers to ensure that your joint efforts promote and boost student learning. Tomorrow's IEP meeting will involve a discussion of another student's needs and strengths, and you'll identify areas that need to be addressed. The portion of the IEP you are responsible for may read something like this:

- Involve the student in a small group on social skills and match the student with a peer mentor.
- Follow up with individual counseling.

The case manager might turn to you and ask, "Would you be able to see the student once or twice a week?" Another IEP team member may ask you, "How would you like me to state the goals you'll be working toward?"

Even with your strong commitment to all of the students in your school, your ever-growing responsibilities may cause you to think, "I can't see this—or any other—student once a week for an entire year! And I wish I felt more certain about determining appropriate goals for this student."

This book has been written to help you meet these challenges proactively with enthusiasm, hope, and a renewed sense of competence. It is a first step toward working *collaboratively* and *effectively* with teachers, parents, administrators, and students with disabilities. The book focuses on higher-incidence disabilities and the student characteristics with which you will most often be faced. The goal is to give school counselors more information about managing those duties as defined by federal law and identified by accrediting agencies and professional organizations, such as the American School Counselor Association (ASCA) and the Council for Exceptional Children (CEC). Throughout this book, we will look at different elements of ASCA's position statement on school counselors and students with special needs. We also recommend that you visit the ASCA Web site (www.schoolcounselor.org) and familiarize yourself with ASCA's Ethical Standards for School Counselors (see Resource C).

Today's school counselors must

- Show that they are proficient with responsive services that are appropriate for typically developing learners
- Show that they can work effectively with students who have a wide range of disabilities
- Understand and address the social, emotional, and behavioral needs of atypically developing learners within the context of federal law and specific school environments

This first chapter provides a brief historical and foundational perspective about how students become eligible for special education and related services. This chapter also highlights laws that affect school counselors and describes multidisciplinary teams and why they are important. Finally, it introduces the broad concept of how schools are federally mandated to respond to students with disabilities and discusses school counselors' unique contributions to these collaborative efforts.

THE INDIVIDUALS WITH DISABILITIES EDUCATION IMPROVEMENT ACT (IDEA)

Students with disabilities include those with a wide range of physical, cognitive, behavioral, and emotional challenges. Such students have varied educational, social, and emotional needs. In attempts to meet these needs, schools may isolate students who receive special education services for part or nearly all of their school day. The Individuals with Disabilities Education Act (IDEA)—introduced in 1975, passed in 1990, and reauthorized in 1997—requires schools and all school personnel to provide appropriate education in the *least restrictive environment* (LRE) for children (birth through age twenty-one) with disabilities. Many experienced counselors may ask, "I wonder if this refers to what I knew as P.L. 94-142 (Education of All Handicapped Children Act of 1975), and IDEA (1997)?" The answer is yes. In 2004, IDEA was again reauthorized, this time as the Individuals with Disabilities Education Improvement Act. Please note that although the word *improvement* has been added to the act's name, this book will refer to the reauthorized bill as IDEA. (The full text of IDEA is available at the National Dissemination Center for Children with Disabilities Web site at http://www .nichcy.org/idea.htm.)

Free and Appropriate Public School Education

IDEA's overall intent is to guarantee a *free and appropriate public school education* (often referred to as FAPE) to all students, regardless of the type or severity of their disabilities. (This FAPE should not be confused with Families and Advocates Partnership for Education, another organization that helps improve educational services for children with disabilities.) This intent reflects the purposes of the previous acts. The new law includes several changes and modifications to the IEP process and other aspects of the identification and evaluation of students with disabilities. Under the new law, planning for postsecondary transition is no longer a choice, and transition goals and services must begin for students at age fourteen. A three-year education plan that focuses on postsecondary goals for students with disabilities should be developed. Secondary students with disabilities who are leaving school are to be provided a summary of their accomplishments along with their final report cards.

This law also speaks to many other specific areas in which school counselors play a part, such as mediation of disciplinary action and parental involvement. The entire text of the law, as well as clear explanations of changes, is available at several excellent Web sites, such as Wrightslaw (www.wrightslaw.com), Reed Martin (www.reedmartin.com), and the National Committee of Parents and Advocates to Protect IDEA (www.spedvoters2.org).

IDEA and School Counselors

Assessment and Placement

Over the years, a variety of special education class placements have been created to help more fully develop the academic and life skills of students with disabilities by providing various levels of support. Placement options ranging from nonschool settings to integrated education in the general classroom (also referred to as *inclusion*) have been used. IDEA entitles eligible students to appropriate evaluations by qualified professionals, and school counselors often play an important role in jump-starting the assessment process. While school psychologists typically conduct psychoeducational evaluations, school counselors are a critical first step in referral and advocacy for student assessment. Parents must give *informed consent* before

> IDEA entitles eligible students to appropriate evaluations by qualified professionals, and school counselors often play an important role in jump-starting the assessment process.

their child is evaluated or reevaluated. However, the law allows an option by which the school counselor can—in rare circumstances—advocate for student assessment and intervention without parental approval. Of course, every effort should be made to work with parents to obtain their understanding and permission.

Inclusion and the Least Restrictive Environment

Due to the implementation of IDEA, more and more children with disabilities have been educated alongside children who are not disabled. At one time, best practice suggested that children with mild learning challenges be educated in the general classroom, whereas students with more serious difficulties were thought to be better served in a resource room or outside of the regular school environment. More recently, this belief has been disputed, and the movement continues to grow to place students with special needs into general classrooms with their peers. Such challenges relate directly to the concept of least restrictive environment, which is another legal aspect of IDEA.

Full inclusion is now the goal of many educators and parents who are leading the special education reform movement. As a result, the 2002 Report to Congress on Implementation of the Americans with Disabilities Act (described later in this chapter) noted that the percentage of students with disabilities who spend more than 80 percent of their instructional time in regular classrooms has more than doubled, from 21 percent to 45 percent. In fact, students with disabilities can be removed from the general classroom only when the nature or severity of their disability is such that even with the use of supplementary aids and services, students cannot be led to success in that setting. While the interpretation of this position may differ from district to district, the overall commitment to greater inclusion is clear.

There are several counseling implications related to providing the least restrictive educational environment for students who have disabilities. First, school counselors may be asked to work with the multidisciplinary team to *develop behavior management programs* for children, as some classroom teachers may not feel equipped to handle the social and emotional behaviors that some students may exhibit. A second implication for counselors is that they will have to *modify classroom guidance activities*, because more children with varying abilities are in the general education classroom. On the whole, school counselors may need to *provide more consultation to teachers* regarding students' affective, social-emotional, or cognitive development.

Eligibility for Services Under IDEA

IDEA includes children and youth with the following specific disabilities as eligible for services, if the disability is determined to significantly interfere with academic progress:

- Mental retardation
- Hearing impairments
- Specific learning disabilities
- Speech and language impairments
- Orthopedic impairments
- Serious emotional disturbance
- Autism
- Deaf-blindness
- Traumatic brain injury
- Visual impairments
- Other health impairments (OHI) such as asthma, sickle-cell anemia, etc., and/or multiple disabilities (National Dissemination Center for Children with Disabilities, n.d.)

Some school administrators may believe that only children with certain cognitive or physical disabilities are eligible for services. Despite the origins of, or motivations behind, this belief, it is far from the truth. Cognitive and physical abilities are only two of several areas in which a child can qualify for services. In one midwestern state, a school denied access to special education services to a student who had a well-documented record of significant behavioral problems and aggression. This student was diagnosed with depression and conduct disorder, but because the school found no cognitive or physical disability, the student was denied services. Lawsuits brought against the school by parents in cases like this have been successful, because serious emotional disturbance is a qualifying condition for services provided under the law.

"At-Risk" Does Not Alone Determine Eligibility

One important aspect to note about eligibility is that a student who has inadequate or interrupted previous education, or limited

English proficiency, cannot, on either basis alone, be considered to have a disability. Learning difficulties due to cultural, environmental, or economic issues alone also do not qualify students for disability services. For example, if a child of a migrant worker is struggling in school, has limited English, and lives in poverty, these conditions do not accurately identify him or her as a student with a disability. Of course, you will work with students with such circumstances as part of your regular counseling duties, but these students will not be automatically placed in special education.

The Multidisciplinary Team

Once it has been determined that a student is eligible for services under IDEA, a multidisciplinary team (called an IEP or child study team in some districts) is formed. School counselors are often the first people with whom concerned parents communicate; as such, counselors are in favorable positions to work closely with all personnel who are providing assistance to students with special needs. Consequently, school counselors will find that their participation as identified service providers to students with special needs and their families will continue to grow.

How and why school counselors get involved in identifying or working with a student who has special needs differs from case to case. But, for various reasons, counselors are increasingly being asked to join multidisciplinary teams in the schools and therefore need to be prepared to take on meaningful and appropriate roles on these teams.

IDEA mandates that a multidisciplinary team must be created when a student has been identified with a special need. Team members must include the following:

- Parents
- One or more classroom teachers
- A special education teacher
- A school psychologist (or an individual who can interpret assessment results)
- An administrator with the authority to make decisions about the student

Other professionals on the team may include a speech and language clinician, a physical and/or occupational therapist, a school counselor, and possibly, at the discretion of the school or parents, a physician. The student is included whenever possible. Together, members of the team pool their assessment results, both formal and informal, in order to make decisions regarding appropriate services for students. IDEA now allows multidisciplinary team members to be excused from participation if a skill area for which they are responsible is not affected.

Collaboration

Collaboration is much more than coordinating services or cooperating with various stakeholders and must be a highly valued part of the IEP process. Collaboration requires each participant to be willing, if necessary, to give up a piece of his or her professional "turf" or control for the good of the larger goal—student success. The idea of a collaborative multidisciplinary team assumes that all participants and their opinions and data are of equal importance, including parents. Each member shares in creating and being accountable for the student's goals.

Experience and research suggest that school counselors may become either over-involved in multidisciplinary teams by acting as case managers, or under-involved by not interacting with very many students identified as having disabilities. An appropriate balance for counselors working with students with special needs is outlined in the American School Counselor Association (ASCA, 2004) position statement (see Resource B).

> IDEA prohibits the exclusion of students with disabilities from developmental guidance and counseling services.

SECTION 504

Section 504 is the section of the Vocational Rehabilitation Act of 1973 that first addressed rights and protections for people with disabilities. According to the statute, in order to be eligible for 504 status, a student must have documentation of physical or mental impairment that substantially limits a major life activity, such as walking, seeing, hearing, caring for oneself, performing manual tasks, breathing, learning, speaking, or working. Naturally, a condition that interferes with learning is of primary interest to teachers and counselors. The law declares that no one should be excluded on the basis of a disabling condition from any program or activity receiving federal support. Most schools receive federal dollars, so they are responsible for complying with this law. The full text of Section 504 is available at http://ericec.org/faq/sectn 504.html.

Section 504 Eligibility

Examples of disabling conditions that qualify for services under Section 504, and which are not typically covered under IDEA, include the following:

- Communicable diseases (such as HIV and tuberculosis)
- Medical conditions (such as asthma, diabetes, epilepsy)
- Temporary medical conditions (such as illness, accident, pregnancy)
- Attention deficit disorder (ADD) and attention deficit hyperactivity disorder (ADHD), though a child with ADD/ADHD may be eligible for services under the category of Other Health Impaired (OHI), explained on page 6
- Drug/alcohol addiction
- Most chronic health conditions (although some may qualify under IDEA, if the condition adversely affects academic performance)

Differences Between Section 504 and IDEA

As noted, any disabling condition that can be documented as *interfering with a student's learning process* may be considered for accommodation under Section 504. This eligibility differs from that under IDEA in that it focuses on equalizing access and eliminating barriers in the regular classroom. IDEA may include significant modification of the curriculum, whereas Section 504 calls for reasonable accommodation within the existing curriculum. Thus, IDEA may require specialized instruction involving a radical restructuring of the learning environment for students with disabilities. Section 504 has to do with allowing students with disabilities to participate fully in existing educational settings

> Under Section 504, reasonable accommodations include allowing more time on a test, or developing an alternative assessment method to replace a test.

without substantial changes. Reasonable accommodations include allowing more time on a test, or developing an alternative assessment method to replace the test. That said, Section 504 defines disability in broader terms than does IDEA. If impairments are determined to limit a student's ability to learn or participate in a major life activity, that student (with ADD, ADHD, AIDS, hepatitis, etc.) may be eligible for services.

Determining Appropriate Accommodations

Appropriate accommodations for each student determined to be eligible under Section 504 are developed by the multidisciplinary team, which includes the parents. Typically, the major responsibility for carrying out these accommodations falls on general classroom teachers. The student's progress, with regard to the goals spelled out in the IEP, is monitored regularly by a Section 504 coordinator. ASCA specifically discourages school counselors from taking on noncounseling-related activities, such as serving as a 504 coordinator. The IEP itself is reviewed periodically (the length of time varies from district to district) to make sure that the goals are still appropriate for the child. Many students who do not qualify for special education services may still qualify for consideration and accommodations under Section 504. Typical accommodations include the following:

- Providing air conditioning in a classroom for students with severe asthma
- Providing voice-activated computers to students with orthopedic impairments
- Offering one-on-one, non-timed testing for students with epilepsy

Another common accommodation in schools is a ramp or elevator. This example is a great reminder of how accommodations prove useful to everyone: Ramps and sidewalk cuts are now used by more people with strollers, wheeled suitcases, and shopping carts than by individuals in wheelchairs.

The intent of the law is to allow all students to have an equal opportunity to benefit from and participate in services offered by the schools. Although the goal is to prohibit discrimination on the basis of a disability, Section 504 does not provide federal funds to support schools' efforts toward that end.

THE AMERICANS WITH DISABILITIES ACT (ADA)

Passed in 1990, the Americans with Disabilities Act (ADA) extends the provisions of the Vocational Rehabilitation Act of 1973 to people with disabilities in public settings, such as employment, parks, and entertainment venues. It is sometimes referred to as the "civil rights act for persons with disabilities." While the ADA is not aimed directly at PreK–12 school settings, there are many school-related implications of this law. For example, Title II of the ADA prohibits discrimination against individuals with disabilities in contexts that include the public schools, vocational education, and higher education. Title II requires that school facilities are physically accessible to all. Title I of the Elementary and Secondary Education Act (1965, 1994) allows school districts to use Title II monies to implement the parental involvement requirements of No Child Left Behind (2002). The National Coalition for Parent Involvement in Education (NCPIE) Web site (www.ncpie.org) provides additional information on this topic. Also, full text of the ADA and much related useful material is available at www.usdoj.gov.

The following case study looks at accommodations that might be made for a particular student. This example and others discussed in this book are intended to illustrate general principles and may or may not apply to specific situations. Eligibility for exceptional student education is ultimately decided by the multidisciplinary team at each specific school and there is an inherent subjectivity in the determination.

A Closer Look: Isaac

Isaac is a seven-year-old second grader with rheumatoid arthritis located primarily in his hands. Isaac has trouble completing some schoolwork and is failing penmanship. He has difficulty participating in art projects and certain physical education activities. Many times he cannot finish tests at the same rate as his classmates. The multidiscipli-nary team determined that the arthritis does not adversely affect his educational performance across the curriculum; therefore, Isaac's dis-ability does not qualify him for services provided under IDEA. Because Isaac's physical impairment limits his participation in school (major life activity) and the limitations are documented via evaluation of his fine and gross motor skills, he is eligible for accommodations by the school district under Section 504 of the Vocational Rehabilitation Act of 1973.

The 504 team, including Isaac's parents, determine that Isaac will benefit from a laptop computer to assist him with written work and some artwork. Occupational therapy will be added, at the school's expense, to help Isaac develop his fine motor skills so that he can participate more fully in art education and improve his penmanship.

When working with children like Isaac, school counselors must be mindful of not only the law, but also their own school district's and state's procedures with regard to these laws. The school counselor will want to be certain that all guidance activities are accessible to Isaac, so that he, too, can benefit from the comprehensive school counseling program.

THE NO CHILD LEFT BEHIND (NCLB) ACT

No Child Left Behind (NCLB) is the educational reform law signed in 2002 by President George W. Bush. It is a revision of the Elementary and Secondary Education Act, which is the primary federal law in precollegiate education (enacted in 1965, reauthorized in 1994). Its stated intent is to increase the accountability of schools, provide more school choices for parents and children, and emphasize basic skills mastery (especially in reading) for all students.

NCLB requires testing of all students with regard to reading and math proficiency. An aspect of this testing that is proving somewhat problematic is the inclusion of students with various types of disabilities in order to monitor annual yearly progress (AYP). While accountability is important and laudable, schools whose students do not make satisfactory AYP are designated as "in need of improvement," or, in subsequent years, "failing." Consequences of failing to meet AYP goals are serious, including possible withdrawal of federally funded supplemental educational services.

On one hand, NCLB is praised as an effort to "ensure all children . . . including those with disabilities, are prepared to be successful, participating members of our democracy," according to the Learning Disabilities Association of America (Harper, 2005, ¶13). In contrast, however, many administrators and parents note that including the scores of students who have certain disabilities with overall school assessment measures can cause those schools to appear to fail.

When first implemented, NCLB allowed 1 percent of special education students to take alternate tests. This has since been raised to 3 percent in 2005, with ongoing discussion of what might be both fair and accurate ways of measuring AYP and school accountability (Council for Exceptional Children, 2005). Over 13 percent of the student population has been noted to have some sort of disability that may impact testing (National Center for Education Statistics, 2004). Students with limited English proficiency (LEP), while previously noted as not qualifying solely on that basis for disability services, are accommodated in the short term by receiving assessments in their native languages. This option is available during the first three years of their schooling in the United States.

The impact of NCLB on schools is immense and the stakes are high. School counselors need to be aware of what is required by NCLB and committed to working with administrators, special educators, teachers, and, above all, students in demonstrating student progress.

Counselors are often involved in testing procedures and help to both prepare students for tests and interpret test results. They may also be active in planning ways to increase student and school success, such as advocating for tutoring services, teaching test-taking

> School counselors need to be aware of what is required by NCLB and committed to working with administrators, special educators, teachers, and, above all, students in demonstrating student progress.

skills, demonstrating relaxation techniques, and so forth. There is no doubt that NCLB is changing how counselors and others focus on the academic achievement of students with disabilities. The full text of NCLB is available at www.ed.gov. For a thorough overview of NCLB and its impact, see the Web site of the Education Trust (edtrust.org).

ADDITIONAL LAWS AFFECTING SCHOOLS AND SCHOOL COUNSELORS

Family Educational Rights and Privacy Act (FERPA)

The Family Educational Rights and Privacy Act (FERPA) is a federal law that protects access to student records. Parents may examine all of their child's student records maintained by the school. Students age eighteen or older may inspect all of their own school records. Schools are required to provide copies, but may charge for them. Parents may ask schools to correct inaccurate or misleading records. Disagreements are mediated during a formal hearing, and unresolved conflicts may result in parents adding statements to their child's records in order to include contrasting information.

Schools must have written permission in order to release *any* information in a student's educational record to anyone other than the student or parents. However, there are several exceptions to this rule, and some include the following:

- School personnel with legitimate interest
- Schools to which the student will transfer
- Accrediting organizations
- Local and state authorities dealing with health, safety, or juvenile justice situations

FERPA rights transfer to students, including those with disabilities, once they enter postsecondary education. The law allows institutions to define what is considered "directory information," that is, what can be released to the public. Some college professionals who work with students with disabilities encourage students to sign release of information forms to the parents immediately. Others believe that this may encourage or continue dependency at a time when students are striving to achieve independence. FERPA does not prohibit students from sharing information with their parents, but leaves this decision in the student's hands (N. Hartenhoff-Crooks, personal communication, August 3, 2006). Full information about FERPA is available at www.ed.gov.

Health Insurance Portability and Accountability Act (HIPAA)

The Health Insurance Portability and Accountability Act (HIPAA) protects the privacy of health-related information. Enforcement of HIPAA is in the hands of the Office of Civil Rights. School counselors deal with issues of confidentiality every day, and HIPAA reinforces that concept in concrete ways. Students with disabilities will perhaps have more privacy issues than other students. Sometimes, even with the best of intentions, school personnel share restricted personal information about a student with a disability in order to explain behavior or alert to treatment in progress.

One of the greatest challenges to student privacy is the use of technology. For example, computers, e-mail, PDAs, voice mail, and the like can give unauthorized access to information that should not be disclosed. Counselors must take precautions, such as password protection, information encryption, and the refusal to transmit sensitive information in public places, in order to safeguard student confidentiality.

WHEN PARENTS, STUDENTS, AND SCHOOL PERSONNEL DISAGREE

Often parents, students, and school personnel disagree about what is best for a child's education and development. This is even more frequently the case when determining the best alternatives for a student who has a disability. When these disagreements occur, IDEA mandates a resolution process comprises three parts: mediation, due process hearings, and appeals to state or federal courts.

Mediation

According to information on the Web site www.wrightslaw
.com, mentioned previously as a tremendous resource for families
and educators, mediation is voluntary, is not used to delay or avoid
a due process hearing, and involves an unbiased, trained mediator
who makes sure that all parties are heard and understood. The
mediator facilitates communication and does not take sides. The
classic book *Getting to Yes: Negotiating Agreement Without Giving In*
by Roger Fisher and William Ury (1991) is a recommended source
of solid information about successful mediation practices.

Due Process

If mediation is unsuccessful, the next step is a due process
hearing. Again, www.wrightslaw.com provides an exceptional and
detailed description of the process. In general, due process is subject
to both federal and state laws and requires full disclosure of evaluations and recommendations regarding the student's school situation. Due process hearings are characterized as adversarial, and can
be compared to medical malpractice suits. Schools must receive ten
days' notice before such a hearing occurs, so school personnel do
have some measure of preparation time. Obviously, it is usually
preferable to avoid such confrontations, and school counselors can
be key in creating solutions *before* family/school relationships deteri-
orate to the point at which hearings are needed.

Family members advocating for the best education possible for
their children with disabilities can be both emotional and highly
motivated. School counselors bring strongly developed listen-
ing skills as well as negotiation skills to such situations, and can
help all parties stay focused on the common goal of meeting the
student's educational needs. Counselors may be able to defuse
power struggles by offering diplomacy and sincere commitment to
a win-win outcome. It is valuable when counselors recognize and
respect the expertise parents bring as educational "managers"
and advocates for their children.

Appeals

From the school's perspective, the worst-case scenario occurs
when mediation and due process hearings fail and formal appeals
are filed with courts at the state or federal level. Counselors must

keep careful records at every stage of negotiation. In the interest of avoiding this final stage of court proceedings, school counselors can facilitate open communication, demonstrate respect, and keep the focus on helping children succeed in school.

The national Consortium for Appropriate Dispute Resolution in Special Education (CADRE) is a helpful source for creating workable agreements between schools and families of students with disabilities. Its up-to-date and user-friendly Web site, www.directionservice.org/cadre, contains a wealth of information, including many resources useful to all parties hoping to reach effective mediated decisions. CADRE urges people to resolve disputes before the safeguard procedures go into effect. Videos, conferences, books, and workshops are among the many tools made available to those who check this site.

CONCLUDING COMMENTS

Since the publication of the first edition of this book (1999), ASCA has expanded and strengthened its stance with regard to counselors working with students who have special needs. ASCA's position statement (adopted 1999; revised 2004) asserts:

> Professional school counselors encourage and support all students' academic, personal/social, and career development through comprehensive school counseling programs. Professional school counselors are committed to helping all students realize their potential and make adequate yearly progress despite challenges that may result from identified disabilities and other special needs. (See Resource B, page 113)

ASCA recognizes that school counselors have increasingly important roles in working with students with disabilities. Some of the tenets of the revised statement that relate to working with students who have disabilities are paraphrased below. According to ASCA, school counselors are involved in (but not limited to) the following:

- Leading school counseling activities for all students
- Providing collaborative services

- Serving on the school's multidisciplinary team that identifies students who may need assessments to determine special needs
- Collaborating with other student support specialists in the delivery of services
- Advocating for students with special needs in both school and community
- Assisting with creation and implementation of accommodations, modifications
- Providing assistance from grade to grade as well as with postsecondary options
- Consulting with staff and parents to understand student needs
- Making appropriate referrals

Further, ASCA delineates administrative duties and decisions that school counselors should *not* carry out, such as making decisions about student placement or retention, supervising implementation of IDEA, coordinating the 504 planning team, and so on. The ASCA Web site, www.schoolcounselor.org, is an excellent source of additional information.

CHAPTER TWO

Specific Learning Disabilities and the School Counselor's Role

The number of children identified with a *specific learning disability* (SLD) continues to increase annually. According to the National Center for Learning Disabilities (NCLD, 2005), almost 2.9 million children in the United States have an SLD and receive some kind of special support in school. Half of the students who are deemed eligible for special education services fall under the umbrella of specific learning disability, most of them in the area of reading. The majority of cases among all students receiving special education services are identified as learning disabled, making specific learning disabilities the most common reason for school-learning problems today.

The Association for Children and Adults with Learning Disabilities (2004) defines specific learning disabilities as chronic conditions of presumed neurobiological origin that selectively interfere with the development, integration, and demonstration of verbal and/or nonverbal abilities. A learning disability exists as a distinct handicapping condition in the presence of average-to-superior intelligence, adequate sensory and motor systems, and adequate learning opportunities. Throughout life, the condition can

> A learning disability exists as a distinct disabling condition in the presence of average-to-superior intelligence, adequate sensory and motor systems, and adequate learning opportunities.

affect behavior, self-esteem, educational achievement, vocational aspiration, socialization, motivation, and daily living activities (2004, ¶2).

In recent years, learning disabilities have been described more broadly as a group of disorders that affect the brain's ability to receive, process, store, and respond to information. Students who show a pattern of unexplained difficulties in doing well academically are referred (with parental permission) for evaluation and consultation.

STUDENTS WITH SPECIFIC LEARNING DISABILITIES: A HETEROGENEOUS GROUP

A counselor might notice during group counseling or classroom guidance activities that students with disabilities may appear inactive or overly active, passive, inefficient, or disorganized. It is vital to pay attention to individual needs and differences. The population of individuals with learning disabilities is extremely heterogeneous. Although one student with a specific learning disability in reading may exhibit low self-esteem and a degree of acting-out behavior, another who qualifies for services in exactly the same way may turn out to be a social leader.

A Closer Look: Suzanne and Jay

Suzanne and Jay are both tenth graders with identified learning disabilities in the area of basic reading skills. Suzanne is shy, withdrawn, and very conscious of her disability. She is at risk for dropping out of school, and when asked about it, says softly, "School's not for me. I'm dumb."

Jay, with the same diagnosis, is outgoing and confident. He is a varsity athlete and has such strong social skills that his learning disability was not confirmed until high school. He is concentrating on learning new coping techniques and is already looking at college catalogs. He likes to stop by the counseling office, stick his head in the door, and say with a winning grin, "I want to do what you do someday!"

This example illustrates the fact that knowing two students with similar, or even identical, learning disabilities does not mean that those students are very much alike. It is especially important that counselors remember that a child with a disability is not necessarily a "problem" student at all, but may require more than one approach to a counseling topic. For example, counselors can honor students' differing needs by designing activities that engage all of their senses. Instead of just talking about how to get along with others, counselors can actively involve students. When the topic is conflict resolution, allow younger students to select symbols made of colorful paper or fabric that depict their feelings. Another option is to ask students to choose from lists of words to express the emotions of the characters in a story. A third example is to encourage students to act out behavioral options by role-playing the feelings that the particular story creates in them.

> Counselors can honor students' differing needs by designing activities that engage all of their senses.

LEARNING DISABILITIES AND RISK FACTORS

While students with many types and degrees of learning disability can be successful in school, the impact of such disabilities on student self-concept can be extraordinary. When you look over the facts below, remember that the vast majority of these students have average or above-average intelligence. Consider what these statistics (NCLD Fast Facts, 2004, pp. 1–2) mean in terms of loss of human potential:

- The high school dropout rate for students with learning disorders is more than 38 percent (compared to 11 percent of the general student population).
- Two-thirds of high school graduates with learning disabilities were "not qualified" to go to a four-year college (compared to 37 percent of nondisabled graduates).
- Only 13 percent of students with learning disabilities attend a four-year institution within two years of leaving high school (compared with 53 percent of other students).

While there is no causal link between learning disabilities and substance abuse, the risk factors are very similar (low self-esteem, academic difficulty, etc.). Another indication of the loss of human potential is the overrepresentation of students with disabilities involved in the juvenile justice system. PACER, the Parent Advocacy Coalition for Educational Rights (www.pacer.org), examines this issue in detail and offers highly useful information. PACER (2004) estimates that 45 to 75 percent of youth involved in the juvenile justice system have one or more disabilities (emotional, behavioral, learning, developmental, etc.). Chemical dependency affects over half of these young people, and dual diagnosis (such as a learning disability with clinical depression) is not uncommon. School failure, limited access to mental health services, and inadequate social skills are among the complex factors discussed at the PACER site.

While no one considers having a disability as reason alone (or as an excuse) for illicit behavior, school counselors must know and act on the fact that students with disabilities are documented as having a much higher risk for getting into trouble with the law. PACER recommends early identification of disabilities, appropriate referral and resources for students with disabilities, use of outcome-based standards, and greater collaboration among families and schools to support students in staying out of trouble.

Another important issue for school counselors to consider is the fact that students with racial and economic backgrounds who differ from the dominant society are frequently misidentified as having disabilities. Many people who work with students who have disabilities have noticed that minority students seem to be overrepresented within that population. This is the case despite strong evidence that students of color are virtually the same in ability level as white students.

Poverty sometimes has an impact on school performance, particularly in regard to contact with toxic substances, nutrition, and other related issues. African American students, in particular, are more likely than other students to be identified as having learning disorders, primarily in high-incidence categories like dyslexia. According to the Education Trust, a somewhat related inequity is the documented under-enrollment of minority students in advanced placement classes taught by the strongest faculty members. School counselors can use their assessment and advocacy skills to critically examine and address these issues in their schools.

> ### A Closer Look: April
>
> April is a 16-year-old Native American student who is new to your district. She is an enrolled member of a Lakota tribe. Teachers report that she seems distracted and cannot keep up in the classroom, especially in math. The school psychologist tests April and finds that her intelligence falls within the average range, and that her mathematics reasoning is at about the eighth-grade level. Under the reauthorized IDEA, a severe discrepancy between achievement and intelligence scores is not necessary for a student to be eligible for services. *Responsiveness to Intervention* (RTI) is the alternative response to IQ-achievement discrepancy for diagnosing an SLD. Therefore, the specific goal with regard to April's lack of progress in mathematics is to identify and understand the nature of her nonresponsiveness to the general education instruction.

At first glance, it may appear that April has a learning disability; however, April was in school only 40 days of her freshman year and skipped an entire semester the following year due to her grandmother's severe illness. The impact of April's missed school days needs to be fully explored before any conclusion is reached. The school counselor's role may or may not include counseling. This student may not have a disability; the school counselor will more likely troubleshoot April's successful re-entry into school. Short-term, time-limited counseling sessions with the school counselor that focus on obtaining a math tutor for April and creating a list of social support contacts may be the extent of the counselor's role in ensuring that April graduates with her classmates.

PREREFERRAL ACTIVITIES

Initial efforts on the part of school staff members to help students who need support to succeed are called *prereferral activities.* School counselors, in consultation with teachers, parents, and specialists, must use problem-solving skills and ask key questions in order to design effective interventions and put them in place (see Figure 2.1; Bangert & Baumberger, 2001).

Figure 2.1   Key Questions for Designing Effective Interventions

1. What is the student doing or not doing that causes us to perceive a problem?

_____

_____

_____

_____

_____

_____

2. Which behaviors should be maintained and which should be reduced?

_____

_____

_____

_____

_____

_____

3. What environmental and/or personality factors contribute to the situation?

_____

_____

_____

_____

_____

_____

4. What is the student's current level of performance and what level will the student need to reach in order to meet expectations?

_____

_____

_____

_____

_____

_____

SOURCE: Reprinted from Bangert & Baumberger (2001).

Prereferral interventions are used for all students experiencing difficulties, not only those suspected to have learning disabilities. Prereferral activities include modifying assignments, arranging for peer tutoring, implementing a contract system, and a host of other options. As appropriate, and permitted by the school district, parents can be highly involved in these activities.

The Teacher Assistance/Child Study Team

The school counselor is typically a member of the Teacher Assistance Team, sometimes referred to as the Child Study Team, and participates in planning and carrying out interventions before a student is formally referred for a psycho-educational evaluation. When a student struggles, either academically or behaviorally, the situation is often brought to the attention of the school counselor. The counselor may work with the student for a few sessions to try to determine the exact nature of the problem and to offer the student small group or individual assistance.

If the strategies implemented at the prereferral stage by the Child Study Team do not bring about improvement, the usual next step is to make a formal referral for assessment. Written parental permission must be obtained before any formal assessment can take place. The school psychologist, speech and language therapist, and occupational and/or physical therapist are among those routinely called upon at this point to provide evaluation. These specialists determine whether developmental delays, specific learning problems, and social-emotional issues exist. School counselors may be asked to conduct observations or provide anecdotal accounts of the contact they have had with the student. If, after referral and evaluation, it is determined that the student is eligible for services under IDEA, an individual education plan is written.

> Written parental permission must be obtained before any formal assessment can take place.

CONCLUDING COMMENTS

Information on specific learning disabilities and their impact on students reveals that there are many opportunities for counselors and other professionals to make significant differences in the lives of students with these conditions. The unacceptably high dropout rate, overrepresentation in the juvenile justice system, and low career achievement of students with disabilities indicate that society is not well served if all of these students' needs are not met early in school. School counselors will be called upon to serve a significant and growing number of students with disabilities. The following list describes the basic characteristics of counseling programs that are committed to effectively including and providing counseling services to students with disabilities. Such programs

- Are committed to the principles stated in the ASCA position statement (see Resource B)
- Support regular counselor collaborations between home and school, and assist all parties in doing what is best for the student
- Encourage students, whenever possible, to accept responsibility for working toward the stated goals
- Put in place a system that allows school counselors to assist families in receiving other available resources
- Include students with disabilities as often as possible in general classroom guidance activities and small psycho-educational group activities
- Regularly assess students for developmental appropriateness of instruction and counseling interventions

CHAPTER THREE

Knowing the Whole Child

Y ou attend the spring choir concert at your middle school and note the range of normal development displayed on the stage before you. Some boys sing bass while some sing tenor; and then there are the self-conscious few whose voices betray them by cracking during every chorus. Some of the young men look as if they are in the fourth grade while others look old enough to shave. Among girls, the range of emotional, cognitive, physical, and social development is just as striking. For example, listen to a group of fourth-grade girls decide how to spend an unscheduled Saturday afternoon. Some of the girls will happily play soccer or dress their Barbies, while others will want to focus completely on boys and practice their already-adept skills at applying makeup.

All of these behaviors fall within the normal range of child and adolescent development. But clearly atypical behavior or development, such as that evidenced by the student who is always alone at lunch or is not involved in any school activity or who consistently acts out in the classroom, might be viewed as revealing a developmental concern requiring your attention. And while it is not always easy to distinguish between the behaviors exhibited by typically and atypically developing children, we increase our chances of appropriate identification of atypical behaviors when we have a good understanding of human development.

GATHERING DATA ABOUT THE CHILD

Data From Others

Many times, the school psychologist or classroom and special education teachers can provide much-needed background data about the student whose name has made it to your desk for additional assistance. This information will be extremely helpful when completing your own assessment of the student.

Gathering Data Yourself

Best practice suggests that the school counselor also gathers information through direct observation, self-report inventories, rating scales, checklists, and interviews. This will help the counselor make decisions regarding special services for the student with whom that counselor will be working. Using various assessment techniques, school counselors should be able to identify areas of concern that are most often connected with a student's social and personal development that can be targeted in an Individualized Education Program (IEP). Behavioral, social, and psychological concerns, such as low self-esteem, inadequate social skills, anger management, or impulse control, that are tied to educational performance, must be measured, addressed, and possibly reassessed later in ways that assure proper delivery of counseling services and follow-up.

> School counselors should be able to identify *areas of concern* that are connected with a student's social and personal development that can be targeted in an IEP.

OBSERVATION AND ASSESSMENT TOOLS

Parent-rating scales, teacher-rating scales, direct observation, structured interviews, and family assessments are practical methods that school counselors can use in identifying specific areas that require attention. Other useful tools include sociograms and genograms. Sociograms help counselors and teachers understand how a student interacts with peers, and how peers view that student. Keeping all responses confidential, a teacher or counselor can generate this information by asking students questions, such as:

- "List the two classmates you'd most like to sit next to in class."
- "Write the name of the person with whom you would enjoy working on a project."
- "If you were going on a vacation, which of your classmates would be nice to have along, and why?" (WikiEd, n.d., ¶ 3. Follow the links for even more information and instruction for creating a sociogram for the identified child and his or her peers.)

A genogram is a type of family tree but involves more than just linking generations. You can also use genograms to map family relationships. There will be a link between a husband and wife, but notation on the genogram can indicate that the couple argues frequently. This information helps to create a more detailed picture of family relationships and issues (see Chapter 6 for an example).

Well-developed assessment tools, both formal and informal, are plentiful. Which ones a counselor chooses to utilize will differ, depending on who refers the student to counseling and the nature of the difficulty that the child is experiencing.

Observations and Interviews

Uncontrolled or naturalistic observations are a good first step, followed by either a structured or semi-structured interview. Having the child and his or her classmates complete a sociogram will provide one source of baseline data that can be documented to begin working with the student on interpersonal skills. The information collected by observing a student's behavior, *when and where it naturally occurs*, can also increase a counselor's understanding of how that student manages the expectations and stressors encountered in the environment.

Jerome Sattler (1998) authored an exemplary book, *Clinical and Forensic Interviewing of Children and Families: Guidelines for the Mental Health, Education, Pediatric, and Child Maltreatment Fields*, that provides school counselors with all of the necessary "do's and don'ts" of conducting high-quality intake interviews with students and their families. This book includes general principles and techniques of interviewing encompassing children and families of color; children with psychological, behavioral, or emotional disorders; and children with disabilities. It presents several fully structured interviews in their entirety. Another excellent source is Stephanie McConaughy's *Assessment to Intervention* (2005).

Formal Assessments

Most school counselors will have the requisite training to use various assessment measures. Master's-level counselors are typically qualified to purchase, administer, and interpret both Level A and Level B testing materials. That is to say, a school counselor, in most cases, is qualified to administer basic and intermediate level tests as opposed to Level C tests (e.g., Wechsler Scales), which require additional training. It is vital for counselors to select assessments that are reliable and valid; that is, matched to the student and his or her area of concern. This is not a case of "one size fits all." It is important to patiently align each and every formal and informal assessment with the appropriate referral concerns.

> Before assessing any child, it is imperative that school counselors who use these various assessment tools have training and supervision that is current and relevant.

Review Tests and Assessment Materials

Counselors should frequently review tests and other assessment materials in order to become thoroughly familiar with the psychometric properties of each. Student scores may determine whether intervention will help the learner become more successful in the school environment. A counselor will want to be convinced that the assessment tool is suitable for the student whose needs are being evaluated. Issues of diversity must be considered. The effects of socioeconomic status, culture, ethnicity, and other such characteristics must be factored into the overall assessment of the child. As noted, students of color are assessed to have disabilities at a rate that is disproportionately higher than that of the general student population. Counselors must remember to carefully review all procedures before proceeding if time has elapsed since the last time they administered a particular rating scale or checklist. If they feel uncomfortable using assessments that are new on the market, counselors may want to ask the district's school psychologist to work with them to help ensure proper administration, scoring, and interpretation. A list of self-report

Table 3.1   List of Assessment Tools

Evaluation Method	General Purpose
Adolescent Anger Rating Scale	Assesses intensity and frequency of expressions of anger in teens
Adaptive Behavior Assessment System, 2nd Edition (ABAS-II)	Assesses adaptive skills functioning
Behavior Assessment System for Children, 2nd Edition (BASC-2)	Measures behavior patterns, emotions, and feelings
Behavior Assessment System for Children, Portable Observation System	Collects social-emotional diagnostic information in a naturalistic setting
Beck Youth Inventories, 2nd Edition	Assesses social and emotional functioning in children and youth
Child Behavior Checklist	Assesses competencies and behavioral/emotional functioning
Child Development Inventory	Reports parent perceptions of child development and symptoms
Piers-Harris Children's Self-Concept Scale-II	Measures self-concept through self-report
Resiliency Scales for Adolescents	Measures personal strengths and vulnerabilities
Social Skills Rating System	Measures social skills in various settings
Student Self-Concept Scale	Measures self-image and academic and social self-concepts
Vineland Adaptive Behavior Scales-II	Measures developmental delays and levels of personal responsibility and self-care

inventories, rating scales, and behavior checklists in Table 3.1 includes many of those commonly used by counselors and psychologists working in schools.

The Behavior Assessment System for Children-2 (BASC-2; Reynolds & Kamahis, 2004b) is a highly respected and widely used instrument that measures interpersonal strengths and perceived academic competencies in various behavioral domains. This assessment includes parent, teacher, and youth report forms.

Many school counselors report that the BASC-2 has proven to be extremely useful in obtaining baseline data for student behaviors and feelings. The following example demonstrates how the BASC-2 can be used to identify children who may have significant emotional needs that are not being addressed in ways that improve their overall school success.

A Closer Look: Hannah

Hannah is an 11-year-old fifth grader who has recently come to your attention. Teachers report that Hannah appears listless, tired, and, at times, unmotivated in the classroom. A review of her grades over the past five years reveals that they are barely passing, except in math, where she consistently maintains a C average. According to Hannah's file, the school psychologist evaluated her in first grade, and the multidisciplinary team then concluded that she did not have a learning disorder.

Based on teacher and parent referrals, a new request has been sent to the school psychologist to repeat the testing. Hannah's mother meets with you and shares her worry that Hannah suffers from low self-esteem and lack of positive peer relationships. The mother also reports that Hannah rarely invites friends over to their home and is never included in birthday parties and other social gatherings. Teachers note Hannah's social isolation as well. During classroom guidance time, you make extra efforts to motivate Hannah to participate, but rarely get a verbal response.

As Hannah's counselor, your next step is to assess Hannah's emotional and behavioral functioning. You may want to administer the BASC-2 and the Beck Youth Inventories, and also conduct a direct observation of her behavior during class and recess. Remember to include a structured interview with Hannah's mother. The school psychologist will assess Hannah's cognitive and adaptive functioning.

Documenting the results of these assessments is important because it helps in the initial phase of the IEP process. The first step is to identify and describe areas of concern relating to the student's present level of performance. Once the counselor has identified the curriculum areas that are affected by the disability, plus the co-existing behaviors and social and personal concerns, an effective plan for counseling and other interventions can be developed.

When assessing a student who presents personal, behavioral, or social concerns, careful documentation of your findings is vital. You will use the data you collect to detail the present level of performance on the student's IEP. Results of these assessments determine whether Hannah qualifies for services under IDEA. A written report of your findings will provide the team with much-needed information and documentation.

REPORTING FINDINGS

Your report begins by identifying the student, the student's date of birth, and the dates the assessments took place. It should include a general statement about the referral concern, the assessment results in understandable terms, and a brief summary of your findings. The next pages provide an example of a short report describing the assessments that might have been completed on Hannah. The school psychologist and other team members (including Hannah's mother) will have conducted their own assessments and provided written reports as well.

Beck Youth Inventories-II

Hannah also completed the Beck Youth Inventories, a self-report instrument designed for children and youth, which contains five stand-alone inventories. Each inventory asks children (defined here as ages 7 to 14) twenty questions related to their thoughts, feelings, and behaviors that directly correlate with emotional and social well-being. In Hannah's case, five areas were explored: depression, anger, anxiety, disruptive behavior, and self-concept. Hannah responded to each statement by marking how frequently she believed the statements were true for her. Hannah's responses indicate that, when compared to other girls her age, she has two areas of clinically significant concerns: depression and anxiety. On both inventories, she scored within the "severely elevated" range. On the other three Beck inventories—measuring anger, disruptive behavior, and self-concept—Hannah scored within the mildly elevated range, within the average range, and in the lower than average range, respectively.

Social-Emotional Assessment

Confidential: Professional Use Only

Name of Student: Hannah

Date of Assessment: 04/27/06

Date of Birth: 07/04/95

Grade: 5

Reason for Referral

Hannah was referred for evaluation by her mother and her classroom teacher. Areas of concern include Hannah's social isolation, complaints of fatigue, and learning difficulties.

Result

Hannah's behaviors as they are perceived to occur within her home environment were rated by having her mother complete the BASC-2: Parent Rating Scales. "[This assessment] is a multimethod, multidimensional system used to evaluate the behavior and self-perceptions of children and young adults aged 2 through 25 years" (Reynolds & Kamphaus, 2004b, p. 1). Children are rated on a four-point scale including the responses of "never," "sometimes," "often," and "almost always." In addition, "the Parent Rating Scales (PRS) is a comprehensive measure of a child's adaptive and problem behaviors in the community and home settings" (Reynolds & Kamphaus, 2004b, p. 4). Between 134 and 160 items are included on the PRS, depending upon the age of the child who is being rated.

Results of the BASC-2 indicate that Hannah's withdrawal, social skills, and somatic complaints are clinically significant. The anxiety and depression scales were scored in the "at risk" range (see Table 3.2).

Hannah's mother's report on the BASC-2 is reinforced by the results found on the Teacher Rating Scales (TRS). The TRS are designed for use in a school environment as a measure of problematic and adaptive behaviors. There are three different teacher forms keyed to the age of the child. The number of questions ranges from a low of 100 for the preschool child to 139 for the child (ages 6–11) and the adolescent (ages 12–21).

Hannah's behaviors, as observed within her school environment, were rated by having her classroom teacher complete the TRS. As Table 3.3 indicates, Hannah's classroom teacher sees her as having symptoms that point to childhood depression. Hannah scored very high on withdrawal behavior, attention problems, social skills, anxiety, learning problems, and depression.

Observation

Student: Hannah

Date of Observation: 01/04/06

Time of Observation: 12:10 p.m. to 12:32 p.m.

Class Activity: Noon Recess

This observation began as the fourth- and fifth-grade students were dismissed for recess following their lunch break. Although Hannah was in the front of the group as it left the lunchroom, she was the last student to leave the building. She walked slowly to the playground area and stood next to the wall of the building. The designated play area includes a basketball court, climbing bars, hopscotch area, and various benches and tables where students play and interact.

During the twenty-two minutes that Hannah was observed, she did not initiate contact with a classmate, another child on the playground, or an adult. When approached by two female classmates, she looked down and shook her head back and forth to indicate that she did not want to join them at the picnic table to look at trading cards. Hannah engaged in no aggressive behavior. When she was not being approached by others, she watched the different groups of children on the playground and appeared to be content to witness their play without wanting or needing to join in. The recess monitor approached Hannah to begin a conversation, but Hannah averted her eyes and answered in one-word responses. Hannah did not speak during the observation period, with the exception of two words to the recess monitor.

The observed behaviors support the mother's and teacher's concerns that Hannah may be isolating herself. However, it does not appear that she is a target for bullying, nor would she fall into the category identified as rejected. She may fall into the subgroup identified as neglected, but, most likely, she would be part of the subgroup identified as average because peers invited her to join them in play. These findings will need to be considered by the multidisciplinary team when putting together goals and objectives to increase Hannah's school success.

Table 3.2   BASC-2 Parent Report Form: Results for Hannah

Primary Scale	T Score	Percentile
Activities of Daily Living	48	40
Adaptability	59	79
Aggression	49	57
Anxiety	76	99
Attention Problems	73	99
Atypicality	51	65
Conduct Problems	44	29
Depression	75	98
Functional Communication	48	39
Hyperactivity	44	32
Leadership	50	49
Social Skills	29	1
Somatization	71	96
Withdrawal	73	97

Table 3.3   Teacher Rating Scales: Results for Hannah

Primary Scale	T Score	Percentile
Adaptability	49	45
Aggression	46	49
Anxiety	76	98
Attention Problems	72	97
Atypicality	60	41
Conduct Problems	44	42
Depression	75	97
Functional Communication	48	42
Hyperactivity	54	76
Leadership	52	57
Learning Problems	73	96
Social Skills	28	1
Somatization	59	87
Study Skills	46	35
Withdrawal	78	98

Self-reports, such as the BASC-2 and the Beck Youth Inventory, can help team members determine the student's overall social and emotional development. You will have results from your own tests and observations to share with the team. Your data, along with that of the school psychologist, parent, and other team members, will provide the information base for constructing effective goals and objectives for Hannah. A student like Hannah will be more likely to lead a successful and satisfying life as her feelings of depression, social isolation, and concerns about learning are addressed. The direct relationship between informed intervention and student success is no longer an unknown.

CONCLUDING COMMENTS

Using and understanding a variety of formal and informal assessments is a key part of the school counselor's role. With the increasing numbers of students who have learning and behavior problems in school, it is absolutely essential that counselors feel comfortable with and knowledgeable in conducting assessment activities.

The assessments listed in this chapter do not comprise an exhaustive list, but they do include those commonly used in schools. Text publishers often offer sample kits at little or no charge. Meet with your school psychologist to discuss which tests to consider and order for use with your students.

You may want to consider making assessment your personal area of focus for continuing professional education. Encourage your local, state, or regional professional association to include experts on the latest assessment techniques and tools in their conferences and newsletters. Ask your school district to sponsor inservice programs for area counselors on this topic. You may even challenge yourself to become the local authority on social-emotional and behavioral assessment. Teaching and consulting with others is a great way to stay up to date. It will also help you accomplish your greatest goal—providing your students with the very best counseling services you can deliver.

CHAPTER FOUR

Matching Data With Appropriate Interventions

The assessment strategies described in the previous chapter provide basic information regarding what school counselors bring to the multidisciplinary team meeting. This chapter links the data gathered and introduces TREAT, a comprehensive model to help counselors conceptualize and put into operation their work with students who are identified as eligible for services.

Once counselors have implemented the TREAT model a few times, they may discover that it gives a convenient and workable structure to what they already do. In addition, school counselors will find this approach extremely useful in both their group and individual counseling with *all* students, not only those who receive special education or 504 services. Another benefit is that the documentation that counselors do as they work through the model will provide more evidence of accountability. By following the model,

> The documentation that counselors do as they work through the TREAT model will provide more evidence of accountability.

NOTE: This chapter is adapted from "T.R.E.A.T.: A Model for Constructing Counseling Goals and Objectives for Students With Special Needs" by R. L. Roberts and J. P. Baumberger, March 1999, *Intervention in School and Clinic*, 34(4), 239–243. Copyright © 1999 by PRO-ED, Inc. Reprinted with permission.

counselors will have a record of their work and evidence that they have met the *minimum standard of care* for their students.

THE TREAT MODEL

Developing realistic goals is always a challenge for the multidisciplinary team. The growing numbers of stressors confronting all students today (e.g., risk-taking behaviors, school safety, and changing family structure) represent additional issues affecting students with disabilities. In response to these challenges, counselors must carefully consider matching the intervention to the area of concern.

Prioritizing effective interventions to match identified and data-supported concerns can be a daunting task. School counselors need to bear in mind all important intervention dimensions for each student, including several that are sometimes overlooked. These sociocultural, environmental, relational, and support system characteristics, as they affect an individual child, are important aspects to review while determining the student's priority educational needs.

> Sociocultural, environmental, relational, and support system characteristics must be considered while determining a student's priority educational needs.

TREAT is a planning model that can be very useful when working with these categories of information. TREAT is a mnemonic device that helps counselors remember all aspects of the model. It guides the writing of goals and objectives toward defensible, realistic, and manageable interventions in five critical areas.

To use the model correctly and most effectively, school counselors must address the areas in the sequence in which they are introduced.

THEORIES AND CONCEPTS

During this first step, a counselor might ask, "How do I conceptualize the student and his or her concerns?" In other words, "Which theories of human behavior and development tell me what to pay attention to with my students, as well as what I can safely ignore?" Counselors are trained to use various theoretical orientations when helping students. These approaches may be based primarily on one

The TREAT Model

Theories and Concepts

Relationships

Environments

Adjunct Services

Treatable Goals and Objectives

> The TREAT model guides the writing of goals and objectives toward defensible, realistic, and manageable interventions.

theory of counseling or may be eclectic in nature. School counselors have found particular success with cognitive-behavioral theories, such as Solution-Focused Brief Therapy and Rational-Emotive Behavior Therapy or Reality Therapy, which is the delivery system for William Glasser's Choice Theory.

Whatever the approach, it is essential that counselors begin with a conceptual model to guide their understandings of students and especially those students who present concerns. Though important, however, theory is not the only part of the conceptualization process.

Personal Characteristics

Larry Beutler and Mark Harwood (2000) believe that at least three key personal characteristics of the student need to be considered when creating the action plan.

- *Problem Complexity.* Is the problem unidimensional or multidimensional? Does the student have a learning disability only, or a learning disability complicated by behaviors and symptoms that are associated with psychiatric diagnoses, such as attention deficit disorder and childhood depression?
- *Interpersonal Resistance.* How open is the student to external influence, especially from adults? Will the student be a reluctant or resistant client?
- *Coping Styles.* How has the student attempted to solve problems in the past? Does he or she internalize by ignoring problems or externalize by acting out and drawing attention away from real issues?

Carefully review and consider the answers you form to each of these questions when creating goals. It is easy to see that students with different coping styles will require different counseling approaches.

Student Motivation

Another issue to consider with regard to problem conceptualization when working on the intervention plan is the student's level of motivation. The degree of student motivation has a major impact on other aspects of the intervention, such as whether restrictive placement is appropriate and who should provide additional assistance for the student. In other words, the lower the student's motivation, the higher the probability that restrictive placement and additional adjunct services will be needed.

A Closer Look: Terrence

Terrence is a seventh grader who repeated the third grade. He falls within the lower range of average intelligence and is identified as having specific learning disabilities in the areas of mathematics and written expression. Teachers and parents report that Terrence is an extremely difficult and draining child to be around because of his endless negativity, passivity, and hopelessness. He has few friends and a history of self-inflicted abuse. The multidisciplinary team requests that the school counselor provide some sort of intervention to get Terrence motivated in at least some areas of his life.

Because Terrence appears completely disinterested and unmotivated, it may be necessary for him to spend a portion of his day in a special education classroom, where he will receive more individual attention from teachers and other staff members. The team hopes to help Terrence find or develop the skills necessary for success with interpersonal relationships and to enhance his academic progress.

One of the first goals in a situation like this is to have a professional on the staff build a close relationship with the student. That relationship will help identify the student's areas of interest, as well as ability levels. For example, a classroom teacher might interpret Terrence's constant looking out the window as a lack of motivation and a compromised attention span. In fact, it may be that Terrence has a fascination with cars and would love to learn how they are put together and what makes them run. This may be one of his few interests, and, once identified, this interest can be used to further motivate Terrence. Reading and math assignments involving auto mechanics may change Terrence's attitude toward learning. Rewards for proactive and self-directed behavior could include time in the auto shop. Although auto repair may not be a core curriculum area, this subject may unlock Terrence's defenses and provide a positive context for school success.

To avoid disappointing setbacks in meeting the goals of the IEP, the counselor will carefully examine motivation, environmental issues, student strengths, and stressors when determining appropriate interventions. Once the larger questions of conceptualization have been explored, three additional questions remain. Typically, the student, parents, teachers, and other school personnel can provide answers to these questions:

- What is happening to the student during school and nonschool hours (social, cultural, and other environmental concerns)?
- What strengths and stressors does the student bring to the counseling process?
- How will these strengths enhance and stressors inhibit the student's meeting his or her objectives?

Additional Testing

Another very important question to ask is whether additional medical or psychological testing is necessary. This question will arise when the basic conceptual questions cannot adequately be answered. At such times, the multidisciplinary team may need to consider requesting additional medical or psychological tests, such as the Children's Apperception Test, Millon Adolescent Personality Inventory, or the Minnesota Multiphasic Personality Inventory–Adolescent.

RELATIONSHIPS

The second major domain in the TREAT model focuses on relationships. As in most counseling situations, the relationship between the counselor and student has a major influence on whether counseling will be successful (Hubble, Duncan, & Miller, 1999). Because this relationship is so important, a critical question must be asked before counseling goals can be written: "Will this student work with me?"

The student's active participation in the counseling process is essential to the helping relationship. Including student hopes, as well as school and parental expectations, enhances the likelihood of success in meeting the identified behavioral and learning goals.

Building relationships with students who have disabilities is no different than building relationships with any other student. Genuineness, empathy, humor, gentleness, sincerity, and warmth are easily sensed and accepted by all

> The student's active participation in the counseling process is essential to the helping relationship.

students. Children and youth are quick to note and appreciate unconditional positive regard, although they would never recognize the term. They also look for congruence between statements and actions, and can "sniff out" a phony fast.

Building a Relationship

One relationship-building activity that works well is to have students create or draw a "yellow brick road" of their lives on large sheets of paper. Ask them to use colorful markers to illustrate important events that have occurred. This is not a one-sided activity; counselors may judiciously participate by completing the activity or demonstrate the activity by using an invented client. If you decide to participate, please keep in mind the ethical issues surrounding self-disclosure and boundary crossing.

When counselors disclose, for example, "This is when my parents had a serious fight in front of me and I noticed . . ." youth tend to respond positively to this level of honesty. Appropriate self-disclosure can provide a model for more open sharing about the student's own life.

A Closer Look: Kelley

Kelley is a 14-year-old eighth grader. Two years ago, she was seriously injured in a car accident. Her father was driving but was not at fault in the collision. Unfortunately, Kelley was not wearing a seat belt at the time. Kelley's spine was broken, and she has lost the use of her legs. She operates an electric wheelchair, exhibits symptoms of depression, and has become argumentative with teachers.

Kelley's family feels terrible guilt about the accident, but also tremendous gratitude that she survived. She is a very intelligent young woman who is now struggling with her academic work (among other things).

(Continued)

(Continued)

Her school records indicate that although she earns above-average to superior scores on standardized assessments, her academic progress over the last two years has become erratic, with classroom grades fluctuating widely. Because of the contrast between her pre- and postaccident levels of academic performance, a psycho-educational evaluation was completed to rule out the possibility of traumatic brain injury (TBI). The results of the tests show that Kelley has no learning disability or evidence of TBI. However, the tests do indicate that she has significant anger and anxiety about her situation and her future. Symptoms of depression are also noted.

Kelley and her parents become defensive when asked about placing Kelley on an IEP to address the emotional consequences of her paralysis and how it may affect various aspects of her life. Kelley's parents think that her only problem is in the area of academic performance. Her father says, "If the school would just be more willing to provide interesting and challenging subject matter, Kelley would do just fine." They believe that Kelley's lack of motivation is due to the fact that assignments and lectures have no meaning or importance to Kelley.

Teachers report that Kelley has constant excuses for her uncoopera-tive attitude and lack of interest in school. They also describe Kelley as resistant, guarded, sarcastic, hostile, and, at times, sad. When teachers intervene with various behavior support programs, Kelley cooperates until she receives her reinforcement, and then returns to her pattern of uncooperative, nonproductive behavior. "She is very capable, but always seems angry," the homeroom teacher says. "I think she has no hope for the future."

Despite several failing grades, Kelley appears to be thoroughly con-vinced that she is doing fine in school. So far, she is not willing to look at how her emotional state or her behavior affects her academically.

Have you worked with a student like this? How will you go about building a relationship with a student like Kelley? Kelley may not realize that, although she is bright, if this pattern contin-ues, she will be in danger of not graduating. Ask her to review the graduation requirements and compare them with her own record. In addition, she may need to experience a different kind of rela-tionship, one with a caring adult who is going to make her accountable for the choices she makes in school, as well as aware of the consequences of those choices. Once this relationship is established, Kelley may be more open to discussing the emotions she attempts to ignore or push out of her awareness.

It is well documented that the therapeutic alliance is more predictive of success than either counselor technique or clinical diagnosis (Hubble, Duncan, & Miller, 1999; Young, 2005). It is difficult to predict what kind of relationship you'll be able to establish before you actually begin to work with a student. However, obtaining information from teachers, parents, and other school personnel, as well as reviewing existing reports, can give you a good idea of what is likely to occur in terms of the student's openness to working with you. Kelley's example is suggestive of what Beutler and Harwood (2000) refer to as interpersonal resistance.

If you get a decidedly positive or negative impression of how the counseling relationship will go, that impression can be reflected in the goals and objectives on the IEP. This is important in order to protect the counselor from being perceived as ineffective. Although Kelley was not eligible for services under IDEA, with students who are eligible you would document the student's openness to counseling under the "present levels of academic, developmental, and functional performance" section of the IEP. This is also noted on the student's initial goals. If the student is likely to spend two months fighting the relationship, you may want to begin with a goal such as, "The student will increase his or her acceptance of the student-counselor helping relationship by requesting a weekly 20-minute appointment and responding to the school counselor positively from 0 percent of the time currently to 80 percent of the time by the end of the semester."

Other questions school counselors might ask regarding the counselor-student relationship include:

- Will the student help create and agree to the goals of counseling?
- What do I like about this student?
- Can I be warm and empathetic?
- Is trust an issue with this student?

The bottom line is to not take the counseling relationship for granted. Carefully consider the relationship's importance with regard to the student and his or her counseling progress and document your findings.

Sometimes the counseling relationship just does not work. In such cases, it is the counselor's responsibility to seek out other options for the student. You may engage another adult helper in the school or refer to a community-based agency that works with children and youth. Abandoning a student client is an ethical violation and something that a professional counselor will never do (Cottone & Tarvydas, 2003; Welfel, 2002).

ENVIRONMENT

The third aspect of the TREAT model involves assessing the student's environment. Questions that need to be asked include:

- Where will the counseling take place (i.e., at school or an alternative site)?
- What mode of counseling will be used (i.e., classroom guidance, group, or individual)?
- How long will it take to meet the stated goals of the IEP?
- How frequently should the student meet with the school counselor or other helping professionals?

Location of Counseling

It is important to answer the first question because, depending on the type, severity, and chronic nature of the problem, the school counselor may or may not provide the service. Students with issues such as suicidal ideation or severely self-destructive behaviors requiring restrictive placement might be referred to an in-patient setting or, at the very least, a therapist who specializes in more severe behavioral interventions. However, students requiring less restrictive environments (for example, a partial pull-out program) could receive services through the school counselor's office.

Mode of Counseling

The mode of counseling must also be selected. Typically, in a school setting, the primary modes of counseling are individual, small group counseling, classroom guidance, or, depending on school resources, family counseling. Most school counselors recognize the need to vary the mode according to the nature and severity of the problem, as well as the availability of support systems and resources.

Duration and Intensity of Counseling

Timing and intensity are the remaining elements that are addressed within this domain. Again, problem complexity and severity, as well as school and student resources, help the IEP team determine how often and how long counseling will take place. If the student with disabilities is experiencing or demonstrating a poor self-concept that interferes with learning, and he or she is open to working with the counselor in small groups, meeting thirty-to-forty-five minutes a week for eight weeks may be appropriate. However, with increased levels of problem complexity, the timing and intensity of counseling may need to be altered. Initial detailed planning will help keep the student, school, and family informed and realistic about counseling progress and goal attainment. To as great an extent as possible, students and other stakeholders need to know when and what to expect so that fewer surprises await them in the course of intervention.

ADJUNCT SERVICES AND SUPPLEMENTAL AIDS

The fourth component—adjunct services—is important because it is often difficult, and at times unethical, to provide counseling to a student without investigating alternative solutions. For example, let's take a look at Irina, a 15-year-old girl who has recently emigrated from Russia with her family. She is failing her classes because she does not read, speak, or understand English well. She has not had the time to make friends and appears lonely. However, she may not need counseling in a traditional sense. Instead, connecting Irina and her family with language classes in the community and support groups through agencies or the religious community of their choice may provide her with all the help she needs to become oriented and successful in her new environment. Another good idea is to pair Irina with a peer helper who will assist her in becoming involved in school organizations and other activities. Counselors can take the lead in modeling multicultural competency within their schools.

Adjunct services may include, but are not limited to, other mental health agencies; legal and financial services; support systems such as family, relatives, or close friends; and community groups. A current and comprehensive referral system will expand available resources and increase the chances of meeting the counseling goals. Many communities provide a resource guide for caregivers and their clients. If your community has this directory, use it; if it does not, create one. Although you might not have time to do this, creating a directory would be an excellent project for peer helpers.

TREATABLE GOALS

The final domain in the model is treatable goals and objectives. This area can be adequately addressed only if data has already been gathered under the first four areas. Failure to consider the variables outlined in TREAT can lead to oversimplified and unrealistic expectations. Unmet expectations can leave both the counselor and the student feeling defeated. The most common example of this is when school counselors rely too much on the relationships built with students and forget that relationships alone do not constitute professional interventions. Counselors who are good at relationships still must conceptualize student issues, create strategies for effective intervention, and set attainable goals.

If, in fact, all of the first four areas have been addressed, then the school counselor can begin the task of writing the student's counseling-related goals and objectives. The next case study illustrates how to determine goals and objectives, and a worksheet is provided for your use (see Exhibits 4.1 and 4.2).

A Closer Look: Jason

Jason is fifteen years old and has been in and out of trouble most of the school year. Jason's mother has already signed the necessary paperwork so that the school district can begin assessing him. The assistant principal encourages her to contact the school counselor to discuss concerns and challenges she has had recently with Jason. She and Jason's father report that they worry about Jason's poor grades and his frequent lying and stealing. They also worry about his fighting, both in and out of school. Because of Jason's behavior, he has been suspended from school three times so far this year.

Jason lives at home with both parents. His father works full-time as a postal worker and reports that he is a recovering alcoholic who has been sober for six months. Jason's father also indicates that, although he has tried, he has never felt close to Jason because Jason has been "trouble from the beginning." However, Jason's father does add that Jason can "fix just about anything" and that he earns his own spending money working part-time at a gas station and garage.

Jason's mother works part-time at a grocery store and spends her free time assisting her elderly parents. She reports having no close relationships other than her parents, her husband, and Jason. She states that Jason "is a good boy" but that he has difficulty controlling his temper and that school has always been hard for him. Both parents report difficulty in disciplining their son.

Jason and his parents agree that Jason experiences frequent periods of depression, often lasting up to three to four weeks. At the time of assessment, Jason reports significant periods of sadness that started approximately two weeks earlier. He has lost interest in school activities that he had participated in, such as wrestling, and he also is not sleeping well.

On the Child Behavior Checklist, Jason's parents report severe conduct problems with his delinquent and aggressive behavior. The severity of Jason's conduct problem is echoed by his classroom teacher. On the Piers-Harris Children's Self-Concept Scale, Jason's score indicates feelings of isolation and loneliness. A review of Jason's cumulative file shows that he has averaged two suspensions per year since the third grade. The social-emotional assessment suggests that Jason has a mood disorder severe enough to be considered an emotional disability. The psycho-educational assessment reveals that Jason is functioning in the average range of intelligence (Full Scale IQ 109), and that he scores in a range considered significantly below his intellectual level on the Kaufman Test of Educational Achievement. These scores indicate that Jason may also have a specific learning disability in the areas of reading and written expression.

The TREAT plan for Jason is shown in Exhibit 4.2.

CONCLUDING COMMENTS

At first glance, the TREAT model may appear time consuming, but only one step needs to be taken at a time. By integrating this model into your counseling practice, you will quickly see that it will help

(Text continues on page 55)

Exhibit 4.1 TREAT Worksheet for Planning

T = Theories and Concepts

1. How do I conceptualize the problem?
   a. Problem complexity
   b. Interpersonal resistance
   c. Coping style

2. Which diagnostic and nondiagnostic variables should be included in the treatment plan?

3. What sociocultural variables and accompanying coping resources are available?

4. Is additional medical or psychological evaluation necessary?

R = Relationships

1. How can I establish a good working relationship with this student?
2. Will this student work with me?
3. What positive and supportive relationships does this student have?

E = Environment

1. Where will the counseling take place?
2. What mode of counseling (individual, group, classroom guidance) will be used?
3. How often will counseling occur?
4. How long will counseling continue?

A = Adjunct Services and Supplemental Aids

1. Social service agencies
2. Legal/financial services
3. Social support systems

T = Treatable Goals and Objectives

1. Have the first four areas been adequately addressed?
2. Can I write measurable goals that are linked to the skill area affected by the disability?

Exhibit 4.2 TREAT Plan for Jason

T = Theories and Concepts

1. Which theory/theories of counseling will I use to conceptualize the problem?

   Initial Stage. Person-centered counseling demonstrating warmth, empathy, and positive regard to counteract authority figure problem

   Working Stage. Cognitive behavioral counseling focusing on Jason's self-defeating behaviors and possible maladaptive thought processes

2. What diagnostic and nondiagnostic variables should be included in the treatment plan?

   Diagnostic

   Conduct disorder (fighting, lying, stealing, truancy)

   Low self-esteem (external locus of control)

   Depression (sleep disturbance and decreased interest in once-enjoyed activities)

   Probable specific learning disability (reading and written expression)

   Nondiagnostic

   Substance abuse in the home

   Overprotective mother

   Long-term problem

   Mother caretaker for elderly parents

   Father known in community as alcoholic

3. What sociocultural variables and accompanying coping resources are available?

   Parents and grandparents

   Successful at part-time job

   Member of the wrestling team (JV)

   Strong mechanical abilities

4. Is further medical or psychological evaluation necessary?

   Request alcohol/drug screening and complete depression assessment

   Review cumulative file for psycho-educational history

R = Relationships

Can a good working relationship be established? Will this student work with me?

1. What kind of emotional bond is possible with this student?

   Freshman and known only on paper

2. Is there agreement on the goals of counseling?

   Working alliance may be tenuous

   Doesn't believe he has any problems but will come to counseling

(Continued)

Exhibit 4.2 (Continued)

3. Is the student motivated?
   Tentatively agrees to work on goals in the IEP

4. Can I demonstrate empathy, warmth, and genuineness with this particular student?
   Authority figure problems
   Pattern of suspicious thinking

5. Is trust an important issue to consider with this student?
   Difficult but critical

E = Environment

1. Where will the counseling take place?
   School (counselor's office)

2. What mode of counseling will be used?
   Group counseling—cognitive behavioral counseling
   Classroom guidance—interpersonal skill enhancement

3. How often will counseling occur?
   Group—50 minutes weekly, staggered hours, so that Jason will miss each class only one time
   Classroom guidance—50 minutes 2(x) monthly

4. How long will counseling continue?
   Until goals identified and agreed upon by the multidisciplinary team are met

A = Adjunct Services and Supplemental Aids

1. What additional services might benefit the student?
   Suggest family counseling to address father's substance abuse
   Suggest Alateen, Alanon, Alcoholics Anonymous
   Counselor will encourage peer support through social skills group

T = Treatable Goals and Objectives

1. Have the first four areas been adequately addressed?
   Yes, but each area will need to be revisited periodically to accommodate new information and personal growth

2. Write goals for the emotional disability (see Chapter 5 for additional examples of how to develop goals):
   Reduce acting out behaviors
   Increase interpersonal skills
   Reduce truancy and suspensions
   Improve mood
   Given Jason's history, his goals may need to be closely monitored and restated so that he can experience some level of school success and improved emotional well-being as a result of the counseling interventions.

(Continued from page 51)

you become thoroughly knowledgeable about the students you are committed to help, and will enable you to be confident in offering recommendations at interdisciplinary team meetings.

In this age of increasing accountability, schools are demanding that their school counseling professionals not only meet with students identified by multidisciplinary teams, but that they demonstrate the skills necessary to successfully work with students who have a wide range of concerns. This can be accomplished best by using a comprehensive model, such as TREAT, which helps counselors determine measurable, manageable, and defensible goals.

Keep in mind that the ways in which counselors conceptualize student issues affects the identified counseling goals and objectives. A systems-oriented counselor would look at Jason much differently than the counselor in the examples provided earlier. From a systems perspective, Jason may be perceived as the family scapegoat. Interventions with Jason would then center on providing coping mechanisms that will help him understand the complex nature of the system he is living in.

Alternatively, a solution-focused school counselor (Guterman, 2006; Metcalf, 1998; Sklare, 2004) might ask Jason to list all the things that are going right in his life and to keep track of all successes. Jason, his parents, and his teachers might learn to pay attention to times when a problem could have occurred but did not and to notice what circumstances surrounded those occasions. The counselor would inquire how Jason solves problems in his life, what works for him, and what he might be able to do to increase those behaviors that he engages in that are also healthy. The technique called the Miracle Question (De Jong & Berg, 2002) might, for the first time, reveal Jason's aspirations and lead to goal setting that motivates him.

CHAPTER FIVE

Building a Structure for Success

This chapter presents ways in which school counselors can identify and work with a student to achieve counseling goals that address the skill or curriculum areas that are affected by that student's disability.

Each state has its own implementation standards for addressing federal special education criteria. Greater numbers of students with disabilities are experiencing academic and social success as a result of state and national efforts to meet these students' needs. School counselors can contribute to these successes by reviewing the guidance curriculum designed for each level of education (elementary, middle, or high school), and making sure that it is inclusive and adaptable for all students. In addition, school counselors can collaborate with their respective principals, special education teachers, and directors of special education to coordinate and advocate for the best possible services for students with disabilities.

IDENTIFYING THE AFFECTED SKILL OR CURRICULUM AREA

One of the first questions to be answered at the planning and placement meeting involves identifying the skill or curriculum area affected by the student's disability. Typically, for school counselors, this involves social-emotional development, career planning and daily living skills, and academic achievement. For example, social competence is a commonly overlooked aspect of student academic success and social acceptance. Appropriate, well-developed social skills are essential for successful participation in school, work, family, and community.

When students experience significant social concerns, learning and quality of life are directly affected. If a student's challenges in the area of social skills are inhibiting his or her academic progress, then social skills should be identified on the Individualized Education Program (IEP) as the skill area (sometimes referred to as the curriculum area) affected by the disability. The law (IDEA) does not require that a student obtain a psychiatric diagnosis to be eligible to receive related services. Counseling is referred to as a related service under IDEA.

> Counseling is referred to as a related service under IDEA.

If a skill area is adversely affected, such as the management of behavior or regulation of emotions, counseling is a legitimate resource for students with disabilities. Related services are included under IDEA so that students with counseling-related needs can have those issues addressed. Once students are identified as eligible under IDEA for counseling services, the school counselor does not need to provide all guidance services on a one-to-one basis. It may be in the very best interest of the student, family, and school that certain aspects of a skill area affected, such as social skills or elements of transitional planning, be addressed through the classroom guidance curriculum already in place.

REALISTIC AND MEASURABLE GOALS

Examples of counseling goals in the social skills area may include the following:

- Krishnan will exhibit increased self-control as demonstrated by accruing less than five detentions per academic quarter prior to the end of the school year. He will increase his self-control by practicing conflict resolution techniques taught by the school counselor during classroom guidance.

- Javier will increase his on-task behavior in algebra from 10 percent of the time to 80 percent of time by the end of the first nine-week period, by participating in the study skills guidance curriculum provided to all students enrolled in high school algebra. The school counselor and classroom teacher will work together to record his progress.

These goals are realistic and measurable. A time frame for accomplishing the goal is identified. The goals also clearly address skills that relate to academic performance and progress. Baseline behaviors can be established, and improvements on these behaviors can be monitored. Finally, these goals do not unnecessarily separate students who are eligible for special education from those who are not. Students with disabilities already spend a greater portion of their time with adults than do other students. More often than not, students with disabilities enjoy learning about themselves, others, and how to navigate the world alongside their typically developing peers.

The social impacts on students who have learning disabilities are well documented; childhood and adolescent social acceptance is a primary predictor of adult social and emotional adjustment. You will recall from Chapter 4 that before school counselors begin to identify and write goals, federal law requires that they document current levels of performance in the areas affected by the disability. If the area affected happens to be social skills, there are many ways to assess this dimension of student functioning. Behavior rating scales; counselor observations; and student, teacher, and parent interviews are widely used for social skills assessment. Once this data is collected, school counselors are ready to co-create goals with the student, the student's family, and other members of the multidisciplinary team.

WRITING SMART GOALS

Goals refer to desired outcomes stated in measurable terms. Objectives are the specific tasks or steps that facilitate reaching those goals. As of July 1, 2005, multidisciplinary teams are no longer required to document benchmarks or objectives for meeting the desired outcome or goal. Therefore, it is vital that multidisciplinary teams write goals that are clear, positive, and measurable.

A helpful device often used in writing strong goals is the SMART model, illustrated as follows.

The SMART acronym helps counselors remember an easy way to check the comprehensiveness of the goals they write for their students. The first two letters refer to two questions: "Are the goals **S**pecific enough to avoid misunderstanding?" and "Are the goals **M**easurable?"

Goals should also include **A**ction-oriented verbs. Make sure that the counseling goals that the team agrees upon clearly communicate what the student needs to *do* to meet the performance that is being monitored. For example, "Tamisha will enter class independently—walking slowly and talking quietly—take her seat, and have all needed class materials with her, four of five morning observations in the classroom prior to the end of the second nine-week period."

The fourth part of SMART reminds counselors to check that the goals are **R**ealistic. This was the major theme of Chapter 4, and by answering questions regarding the first four areas outlined in the TREAT model, goals will be not only realistic, but also affirming and effective.

Finally, are the goals **T**ime oriented? In other words, does the goal contain a specific time frame to accomplish the progress that is being sought? Will parents or caretakers receive a *descriptive* written report covering the progress their child is making toward the goals agreed upon early in the school year?

If school counselors are to adequately and responsibly meet the needs of students, all five of these critical questions must be answered while the goals are being written. Thinking SMART is central to creating goals that are both measurable and manageable.

The Importance of Writing Your Own Goals

School counselors must be actively involved in creating the goals in areas that they will be responsible for carrying out. Occasionally, however, case managers, administrators, and special education teachers write goals for counselors without consulting them, and then inform counselors of what they must do. A real-world example is an IEP that read, "The school counselor will meet with Abby daily from 1:00 to 2:00 p.m. to increase her self-esteem."

This example is problematic on at least four levels. First, to schedule an individual counseling commitment in such a way puts the school counselor in an impossible dilemma! Schools are legally obligated to provide any services written into an IEP, and this level of obligation is rarely possible to honor. Second, professional school counselors know that it is not therapeutically sound for them to work with a young child individually for an hour each day. Third, this level of attention to one student also means that many other students will go without counseling services. Fourth, this is a poorly written goal. There is no mention of what the student will do, the baseline behavior, or how much change is expected and by when. The entire situation is fraught with ethical and technical problems.

> Counseling goals must directly relate to the needs of the student and skill areas affected. Goals should be selected in terms of their achievability, involve remediation and not rehabilitation, and specify the intended counseling outcome in measurable terms.

Appropriateness of Goals

Goals need to be written in such a way that they reflect sound therapeutic judgment. Rather than state that the counselor will improve self-esteem by working with Abby once a week for the entire school year, state that

> After participation in a four-week guidance unit focusing on personal strengths, cooperative behaviors, and positive peer feedback, Abby will identify her specific talents, and give and accept positive feedback from peers as reported by Abby.

Additional examples of counseling and guidance goals are presented later in this chapter. Some are very specific and others are more general. School counselors will need to work with special education teachers to determine how much detail is required in specific school districts when writing goals that will satisfy IEP documentation requirements.

Appropriate Duration of Service

Duration of service is another element that must be addressed on the IEP. It is reasonable to expect that counseling goals will be reviewed frequently to reflect student gains and also goals that have been met. The multidisciplinary team may also call a meeting (although it is not required) or a team member can work with the parent or guardian to write an addendum that dismisses the student from counseling services identified on the IEP once the goals are accomplished. The student will continue to participate in the guidance curriculum with his or her peers who do not have disabilities, but without the need for special education documentation.

Reed Martin (2006), an attorney and expert in special education law, maintains a Web site (www.reedmartin.com/iepgoals .htm) where he suggests that a goal should include the following:

1. The intended direction of change (increase/decrease)

2. Specific concerns (off task/biting/truancy)

3. The present level of performance (no demonstration/ partial demonstration)

4. Quantity or quality of growth (demonstrates 90 percent of the time)

5. Specific intervention to promote the change (group counseling)

Remember that counseling goals must directly relate to the needs of the student and skill areas affected. Goals should be selected in terms of their achievability and specify the intended counseling outcome in measurable terms.

Table 5.1 illustrates the present levels of performance and measurable goals to be set for three students whose disabilities affect the social-emotional learning curriculum area. Although the counselor may have been identified as the primary person responsible for carrying out the goals, others who are involved can and should be charting observations. All parties (e.g., teachers, support staff, and parents) can help to document that the guidance curriculum or responsive services are producing the behavioral changes stated in the IEP.

CAREER-RELATED GOALS

In the area of career development, counselors play an integral role in successfully transitioning students from schoolwork to paid work. Students with disabilities are at great risk for unemployment upon

Table 5.1   Matching Current Functioning to Goals

Present Level of Performance	Measurable Goals
Strengths. Based on teacher and parent reports, Sara draws and paints very well. Sara takes pride in her artwork. Sara is making adequate progress in the mathematics curriculum. Sara is polite and well mannered.	*Goal One.* Through participation in the sixth-grade class guidance program (social-emotional learning), Sara will achieve a healthy balance between time spent alone and time spent with others. This will help her to decrease feelings of rejection and increase feelings of acceptance by self and others as measured by the Beck Youth Inventory (self-report) and parent report.
Needs. Based on counselor interview, parent and teacher behavior ratings, and student response inventories, Sara demonstrates an attitude of hopelessness, loneliness, isolation, and a general sense of worthlessness. Based on observation, Sara withdraws and isolates herself in the classroom and lunchroom. Sara is not making acceptable progress in the reading curriculum.	*Goal Two.* Sara will initiate and engage in conversations with school personnel to demonstrate continuous improvement in the social skills curriculum as measured by the classroom teacher and parents. For example, when given a verbal greeting by school personnel and/or classmates, Sara will respond by giving a greeting back during three of four observations for six consecutive trials.
Strengths. Parents report that Tommy is very organized and takes good care of his possessions. Teachers describe Tommy as a social child who volunteers to help whenever an opportunity becomes available. He is also athletic and excels at basketball and baseball.	*Goal One.* After individual counseling using demonstration and role play, Tommy will accept directions from his teacher by behaving courteously, following rules or requests ("please be quiet"), or modifying his behavior with 70 percent compliance.
Needs. Counselor observation noted Tommy fails to take turns, talks out of turn, loses his books, and breaks classmates' belongings. Teachers report that Tommy is easily distracted, does not complete his seat work, and is in and out of his chair often. In the area of conduct he often receives a check mark under "needs improvement." He is referred to the office several times a week for rule violations. These behaviors are inhibiting his ability to make standard progress in the fourth-grade curriculum.	*Goal Two.* The number of Tommy's disciplinary referrals will decrease from three each week to one each month by the end of the school year by learning self-control and anger reduction strategies taught through the social skills curriculum in a small group counseling format.
Strengths. Eli is a good-natured young man and is extremely polite. He is one of the best math students in the second grade. He performs well in art, penmanship, and story writing. He is proud of his work and does not turn it in until he declares it "perfect."	*Goal One.* Eli will use one of two coping strategies (self-instruction and self-monitoring) he learns in small group counseling to block and delay self-harming behavior from five each day to two each week by the end of the school term.
Needs. According to Beck Youth Inventory, Eli tends to become overwhelmed easily. His teachers note that when offered corrective feedback by parents or teachers, he cries, pulls his hair, and pokes himself with a pencil.	*Goal Two.* Eli will demonstrate that he can use relaxation techniques learned in classroom guidance to reduce the overall frequency and intensity of his current responses to anxiety in and out of the classroom as observed by teachers and parents.

graduation. The National Health Interview Survey conducted by the Office of Disability Employment Policy found that 79 percent of adults without disabilities were working at the time they were interviewed, and only 37 percent of those with disabilities were employed (U.S. Department of Labor, 2005).

IDEA is clear in its expectation that students with disabilities will receive assistance in preparing for productive adulthood. School counselors have considerable expertise in career development and can offer key leadership in this area. However, counselors need to know how certain disabilities may influence physical, social-emotional, and cognitive development while always keeping in mind the wide range of individual differences possible. Rehabilitation counselors are allies in this process and can connect students with resources and services that are intended to help them.

Sometimes counselors must manage the delicate balance between encouraging realistic goals and discouraging unrealistic ambitions. Pete, for example, is a tenth grader with cerebral palsy. He would like to become either a firefighter or a police officer. These careers require passing rigorous physical examinations that he may never be able to master. However, Pete may well be able to become a very competent dispatcher or 911 operator. In this way, he can be encouraged to work in the career area he finds exciting, but within a role in which he can become highly successful. School counselors need to be aware of alternative career assessments, prepared to modify their own career materials, and ready to assist students with interest surveys that are sometimes beyond their reading or comprehension level. The following case study is one example of how career development goals can be written into an IEP for a student with developmental disabilities.

A Closer Look: Molly

Molly is a 16-year-old African American girl with Down syndrome. She is shy but once she becomes more familiar with others, her lively personality emerges. Despite her introversion, Molly cares about her appearance and especially likes jewelry. She likes to try different hairstyles and colors of nail polish. She lives at home with her family, and is the youngest of three children. Both of Molly's parents work outside the home. Molly comes from a close-knit family where she is accepted and well loved.

Although she can stay in the public school until age 21, Molly's parents are looking ahead to the time when she can move to a group home and retain a job with supervision. Her parents are making contact with appropriate resources and agencies in the community and are active participants on the multidisciplinary team at school.

Molly is excited about learning how to earn her own money. She looks forward to graduating from school and leaving home at some point. She would like to live with other young people and will accept a supervised group home as one possibility.

The school counselor needs to be aware of issues beyond Molly's developmental disability. Racial and gender issues may also influence her future. Since Molly is a friendly but naive young woman, safety issues will need to be addressed before she leaves school. The school counselor needs to determine where these issues can be dealt with in the comprehensive school guidance program. As a general goal, the counselor may suggest that Molly identify an appropriate career direction, including adequate knowledge to obtain and maintain a job (with support as needed). If the multidisciplinary team agrees that Molly's career choice is an appropriate goal for her, it can then determine that the school counselor, the special education teacher, and Molly's parents will all be responsible for helping her achieve it. Table 5.2 lists additional goals for Molly to accomplish before the end of the school year.

LIFE-SKILLS GOALS

Students with disabilities often need assistance in acquiring skills for independent living. These skills can range from learning how to set up a checking account to how to behave acceptably in public. People with certain disabilities suffer from discrimination and the judgment of others, sometimes simply for the peculiar but harmless ways they conduct themselves. For example, a young woman was arrested for public intoxication, when in fact, her unbalanced gait was caused by a physical disability.

Students with disabilities can display many kinds of behavior that can be viewed as unusual. Some of these include head banging, rocking, clapping, making unusual noises, shadowing,

Table 5.2   Molly's Goals

Present Level of Performance	Measurable Annual Goals
Strengths. Molly is interested in obtaining a job and eventually living away from home. She has a willingness to try out new ideas and experiences with support.	*Goal One.* Molly will expand her choices of potential employment sites through participating in and completing all activities in a six-week career exploration class. Molly will be able to list three jobs she may like and three jobs that she is not interested in pursuing.
Needs. Parents report that Molly has responsibilities in the home but has no real knowledge of how to get and keep a job.	*Goal Two.* Molly will demonstrate increased job acquisition skills. Following instruction on job applications and interviewing etiquette, Molly will role play with a nondisabled peer helper during high school guidance time; learn how to complete a modified job application form; and independently enter a work site, drop off an application, and speak clearly to the people who greet her.
	Goal Three. Molly will tour at least two job sites and meet with people who do jobs she might be interested in and able to perform (e.g., food service, cleaning, filing, or manufacturing). When asked, Molly will respond to work-related questions with 100 percent accuracy in four out of five trials. For example, when given a work schedule and transportation schedule, Molly will state correctly at least four out of five times what time she must leave home to arrive at a work site within 10 minutes of the time she needs to be there.

running in circles, and picking at skin. In addition, due to frustration or inability to be understood, some people with disabilities will occasionally throw violent temper tantrums. School counselors will want to become familiar with this full range of behavior so that they can help teachers, students, and parents understand that these behaviors may be part of the disabling condition. There is a danger that students who behave oddly will be misdiagnosed or further labeled as seriously emotionally disturbed. It is important to remember that although all children may exhibit unusual behavior from time to time, some students with disabilities will exhibit these behaviors more often or with more intensity.

> ### A Closer Look: Henry
>
> Henry is a 12-year-old sixth grader who has a hearing impairment and is developmentally disabled. He lives at home with two older brothers and a younger sister. His father works long hours and his mother is a full-time homemaker. Henry loves his two cats and spends a lot of time grooming them. His grandmother, who lives nearby, has taught Henry how to work with clay, which is his favorite hobby.
>
> In the last six months, Henry has exposed himself on the playground and attempted to sexually stimulate himself in the resource room. Some classmates tease Henry about his behavior, and many others just avoid him. Henry is confused by these reactions and his lack of acceptance. He does not understand that what he is doing is not socially acceptable.

It is the school counselor's responsibility to be aware of Henry's increasing isolation and attempt to quickly and effectively address it to avoid long-term, negative consequences. An appropriate goal for the multidisciplinary team might be:

> Through participating in the *Good Touch/Safe Touch* unit for middle schoolers, Henry will increase appropriate and decrease inappropriate physical touch of self and others.

If the team agrees this is a suitable goal, team members can work together to create benchmarks toward related goals that are specific, measurable, action oriented, realistic, and time specific.

CONCLUDING COMMENTS

This chapter has shown how SMART goals can be constructed. School counselors who are responsible for implementing the goals must also be involved in creating them. It should be a common practice that school counselors advocate for students with disabilities, as counselors do with all other students. Two ways to do this effectively are to be actively involved in any counselor-related goals identified by the multidisciplinary team and to readily be able to modify the guidance curriculum so that all students can successfully participate.

Guidelines and requirements for writing IEP goals vary considerably from district to district and are, in any case, a challenge to establish. Counselors should consult with other behavior specialists from time to time for correctness and accuracy in goal writing. Remember that goals must be therapeutically sound and fit within the overall mission of the school. Your expertise and creativity as a counselor will be tested when it comes to writing good goals and objectives!

CHAPTER SIX

Forming Partnerships With Families

W orking with parents and families of students with disabilities can be both wonderful and challenging. Students who experience social-emotional problems in school do so not in isolation, but rather within the context of the family and other social systems. The school itself is a system into which students bring the values, ideas, and interactional patterns of their family systems. Students with disabilities affect both school and family systems and are, in turn, affected by them.

Both these systems resist change and try to maintain their own internal balance. Just as people have roles in their families, they also have roles at school, and it is wise to remember that efforts to effect change in either of these realms may be ignored or even sabotaged. When thinking from a systems perspective, it is vital to involve all members of both systems in trying to bring about positive change.

PARENTS AND FAMILIES AS EQUAL PARTNERS

As counselors are aware, parents (including legal guardians and surrogate parents) should be encouraged to participate as equal partners in their child's education. However, parents of children with disabilities often have distinct and significant reasons to be involved at school. These parents bring specific, valuable knowledge of their child's uniqueness. They also bring a longer-term perspective on their child's development. For instance, a high school student experiencing attitude problems and struggling academically because of a head injury may be seen by school personnel, who may not be fully aware of the student's situation, as suddenly combative and disrespectful. A visit with the parents may reveal adjustment issues dealing with grief due to the injury, a sense of powerlessness, and severe loneliness. This information can shed new light on the student, who then may be viewed more fairly and supported in more effective ways.

> Parents bring specific, valuable knowledge of their child's uniqueness. They also bring a longer-term perspective on their child's development.

By law, parents must be included in all decisions regarding the special education needs of their children. Parental involvement is more than a courtesy—it is mandatory under IDEA and Section 504. Parents must receive written notification of any alterations in their child's educational program, a procedural safeguard that is guaranteed to all families. This notification must be provided for any Individualized Education Program (IEP) meetings, reevaluations, or when a parent requests a due process hearing. The school counselor and the multidisciplinary team should view input from parents as positive opportunities. Parents, after all, have the highest stake in their child's success.

Families have tremendous influence on the degree to which their children are successful at school. Working with, educating, and learning from families is a good investment of a school counselor's time and energy. Parents who support guidance programs feel more favorable toward the school and their child's education than those parents who are less aware of the counseling curriculum. There is a positive correlation between family involvement and student success, regardless of disabling conditions (Taylor, 2000). School counselors can be the link for encouraging family involvement in the schools.

Parents are often waiting for an invitation to become more involved with their child's schooling. Questions counselors can ask themselves in this regard include the following:

- How can I help the families I work with feel like equal partners in their child's education?

- How can I help parents feel welcome in our school?
- How can I help teachers and parents see the benefits of working together?

These questions are perhaps even more vital to address with parents of students with disabilities. Of course, not all of the responsibility for good school-family relationships falls on school counselors alone. Some parents may not know how to best interact with school personnel or realize the extent and nature of assistance available from school counselors. ASCA (www.school counselor.org. Click on "Parents & Public" and then "Back-to-School Tips.") shares five clear recommendations for parents who would like to build good working relationships with school counselors:

- Find out what school counselors are and what they can do to assist your child.
- Communicate with your child's school counselor at least three times each year.
- Let your school counselor know about your child's individual concerns and challenges.
- Use your school counselor to find out about school policies and procedures, as well as community resources that may help your child.
- See your school counselor as a partner in your child's success (ASCA, 2005b).

It is a good idea to make these points available to parents either during orientation or in a handout or via the school Web site, in order to enhance communication between parent and counselor. And again, it is especially important for parents of children with disabilities to gain these perspectives on working with counselors.

Relationships between parents and schools can play out in many ways. Power and Bartholomew (1987) have written about the following five types of school-family relationships still prevalent today:

- The avoidant relationship ("Let's just not deal with each other.")
- The competitive relationship ("I'm the expert here!")
- Merged relationships ("I almost feel like I work here, too!" or "I almost feel like Rosa's 'other mom.'")
- The one-way relationship ("I'll do whatever you ask.")
- Collaborative relationships ("Let's work together to help Andrew have a great transition to middle school.")

Knowing about these types of relationships can help school counselors identify, better understand, and improve the nature of the relationships that they observe and participate in with children's families.

It may seem at times that there are only two types of parent-school relationships. In the first, the parents see school professionals as the experts and back off in their level of involvement, as in the one-way relationship just noted. In the second, high parent involvement is seen by school personnel as enmeshment (or the merged relationship) and is disdained.

FAMILY FUNCTIONING

There are many ways to look at family functioning. One way is to look at family boundaries. When school counselors work with families, their questions can explore and discover whether the boundaries are rigid (i.e., very private) or diffuse (i.e., very open). Another quality to examine is the adaptation skills of the family. How does it handle stress or change? Cohesion refers to togetherness versus autonomy among family members. Disengaged families are said to have low cohesion. In contrast, connected families value family closeness but also allow each member some degree of independence. Enmeshed families have too much togetherness and members have difficulty functioning as individuals (Fenell & Weinhold, 1997).

Here is a scenario, taken from an elementary school, that might look like enmeshment to a school counselor. A boy who uses a wheelchair and is sensitive to the cold is observed as always being attended to by his younger brother on the playground before school and during recess in the winter. The younger brother adjusts the mittens, hat, and scarf of the older wheelchair-bound brother and never leaves his side. When the bell rings, the younger boy escorts his brother not only into the school, but also into the classroom, before continuing to his own class. The boys' father calls the school every day to make sure that his son in the wheelchair is safely inside. School staff might easily conclude that this family is over-involved in the welfare of the child with the disability to the point that this child's independence and sense of self-reliance could be threatened. But is it enmeshment? Or has this family, as a result of a negative experience at school that left the boy in the wheelchair out alone during an extremely cold winter day, found a way of managing the situation using its own resources?

In the situation described here, the school counselor should look carefully to see if the closeness is, in fact, inhibiting the development of the older child. It seems more likely that the family is showing appropriate concern for a child they see as vulnerable, and taking care to make sure he is safe and warm.

MAKING PARENTS FEEL WELCOME

Unfortunately, parents often feel unwelcome, intimidated, or even blamed when they attend meetings at school. Sometimes this is because they themselves had negative experiences when they were in school. For example, there is evidence that certain learning disabilities are inherited. Parents who, unlike their children, were undiagnosed and perhaps seen as problem kids in their own day, may relive feelings of frustration or inadequacy when returning to the school environment to deal with their own children's issues. They may consciously or unconsciously resent a system that did not help them when they were in school. In contrast, many parents of students with disabilities were successful, even superior, students when they were in school. These parents can be shocked and disappointed if current experiences with their children seem to be in great contrast to their own positive school experiences. Regardless of their educational histories, all of these parents must be shown that they and their children are not in trouble. Parental involvement is essential in creating the best possible learning environment for children. How different would it be at school if parent conferences were truly regarded as collaborative, instead of mandatory, or even punitive?

> All parents must be shown that they and their children are not in trouble, and that parental involvement is essential in creating the best possible learning environment for children.

If you pick up on negative parental feelings about school, suggest that parents bring a friend or another family member with them to the meetings. Be sure to frame questions in positive ways whenever possible: "What would you like us to know about Timothy?" Always use respectful language (Mr., Mrs., Ms., Dr., etc.), and always refer to the student by name.

Parents will feel welcome at school if they are encouraged to visit when school is in session; they can, for example, stay for a planned lunch with their elementary school-age child. If having parents present at certain times in the school day is disruptive, rules for these visits should be negotiated honestly and in good faith.

Family Experiences With, and Expectations of, Schools

Most parents of children with disabilities have an exhaustive history of trying to get school personnel to understand their children's needs. They are likely, in fact, to have had some unpleasant experiences while trying to find the best possible school environment for their child. They may have experienced active or passive resistance on the part of teachers, counselors, and principals, or they may have perceived resistance in cases where there was only misunderstanding. It is good to remember that these parents often feel, for good reasons, that they are the only true advocates for their child.

One common source of misunderstanding and conflict in this area is that schools are required to provide only an *appropriate* education for the child, which is not always the most optimal one. Parents, quite understandably, want the very best for their child, whereas schools have only limited resources that are meant to meet the needs of all the students.

School counselors can be pivotal in establishing good working relationships and mutual trust among parents and school personnel. Counselors can be the ones who explain the assessment and placement process to the parents. Parents often receive only a brochure or folder of confusing material before coming to their first IEP meeting at school. This is not a good way to build an open, trusting relationship. Many parents may arrive feeling mistrustful or anxious about whether the child will be able to succeed in that school. Often, their previous efforts to get services for their children at school have made them pessimistic. One of the roles of the school counselor is to acknowledge and address the legitimacy of parents' frustrations.

In a terrific essay titled "Hope for Special-Need Students and Their Parents," available on the ASCA Web site (www.school counselor.org. Click on "Parents & Public" and then "Articles for Parents."), Drs. Rita and John Sommers-Flanagan (2006) recognize what parents bring to the education of their children with disabilities:

In our opinion, no other group of parents is as dedicated to their children's academic opportunities, social and emotional development and overall well-being than parents of children with special needs. Typically, these parents have spent years advocating for their children. This is exhausting and often unrecognized and underappreciated work. (¶2)

School counselors who incorporate the wisdom of this statement will increase their chances of success with students who have disabilities and their parents.

A Closer Look: JaMarr

JaMarr is a high school junior of average intelligence who is eligible for special education services because of his inability to monitor his mood disorder. This interferes with his academic progress in the core curriculum areas of math and reading. The immediate issue is that JaMarr is not turning in his math homework. He is reportedly uncooperative about doing these assignments as well as chores at home.

As a single parent with two other children, JaMarr's mother is having a hard time getting him to complete his homework. The resource room teacher came up with a plan to help him catch up. This plan required JaMarr to come to the resource room after school for forty-five minutes, Monday through Thursday. According to his mother, neither she nor JaMarr were given any input into the plan, nor were they asked for suggestions on how to solve the homework problem before the plan was presented to them at a meeting with the resource room teacher. Since JaMarr's mother did not know what else to do and she did not want her son to fail, she agreed to the plan. JaMarr also agreed in the meeting to try it. They recognized that the resource room teacher wanted to help.

But things did not go well. JaMarr often arrived late to the resource room after school and lingered in the hallways, chatting with friends, as long as possible. He started complaining to his mother about "feeling like I'm in detention every night." The mother relayed this information to the resource room teacher, who in turn became defensive. One afternoon a few weeks later, JaMarr did not show up at all. The resource room teacher asked a paraprofessional to track him down. The paraprofessional found JaMarr and ordered him to the resource room. Unfortunate words were exchanged. When JaMarr finally arrived in the resource room, he again used inappropriate language and was belligerent. The resource room teacher—a small female—felt threatened. She made an office referral, which led to JaMarr's suspension.

═══════ (Continued) ═══

> (Continued)
>
> JaMarr's mother called a parent advocate whom she asked to accompany her to a school meeting concerning her son's behavior. The meeting started badly, with the mother attacking the plan in angry, direct language. The teacher immediately defended the plan, pointing out that both mother and son had signed it. The dispute continued, with no solution in sight.

JaMarr's situation, while not an easy one, is not infrequent, either. When a plan goes awry and parents and school personnel come to a stalemate, it is critical that the school counselor step in, perhaps by trying to unite everyone with a question such as, "Can we all agree that the plan isn't working?" If there is agreement (and in JaMarr's case, there should be!), something new can be tried.

Arriving at conflict resolution in this situation involves refocusing on the original objective: getting JaMarr's homework done and turned in. In JaMarr's case, the school counselor noticed that JaMarr was taking a PE class, although he had enough PE credits to graduate without it. She also noticed that JaMarr was paired with an inexperienced algebra teacher. With the consensus of the group (including JaMarr), the decision was made to have JaMarr drop PE and add a study hall. JaMarr was also moved to Mr. Luking's algebra class. Mr. Luking was a more experienced teacher with a master's degree in mathematics education. He taught both general and advanced placement math courses and offered extra help two afternoons a week. With these changes, JaMarr had time for homework during the school day and could also get help in math as needed from a strong, experienced teacher.

Working Strategically With Families

Lockhart (1998) suggests using Jay Haley's model for Strategic Family Therapy in running IEP meetings. Counselors can incorporate the strategies suggested by the model and encourage others involved in IEP meetings to use this approach as well.

The Haley model consists of six phases. The first phase begins the meeting with social conversation designed to reduce tension. What is sometimes undervalued as "small talk" can actually be a good way to connect with parents. Set the stage for good communication with brief personal comments that build a bridge:

"Thank you for coming, Mr. and Mrs. Williams. I've been looking forward to seeing you again. Would you like a cup of coffee?"

In the second phase, goals for the meeting are presented. This is a good time to again mention the Family Education Rights and Privacy Act (FERPA; U.S. Department of Education), which states that parents have the right to a copy of any written information about their child.

The third phase is the problem stage. Counselors could refer to it as the presenting concern stage. At this point, all meeting participants share their perspectives on the issues under discussion while the other meeting attendants listen. Questions are not encouraged until everyone has had a chance to speak.

Fourth, the group discusses what has been presented and gets clarification where necessary. In this phase, any and all questions are raised and talked over thoroughly.

In the fifth phase, the team develops an appropriate plan for the student, capitalizing on his or her strengths and addressing areas of need.

Finally, in the sixth phase, tasks for meeting the goals and objectives are assigned. Consensus and mutual respect are sought throughout this process. Parents have the right to challenge information in the student's educational record, as well as to add corrective data or opinions.

EARNING PARENTS' TRUST

What can counselors do to earn the trust of parents? As mentioned earlier, they can treat parents of children with disabilities as equal partners with a full range of strengths, weaknesses, and resources, who are also doing their best to manage with a child who has a disability. It is important for counselors to prepare for each meeting, to try to anticipate parents' questions, and to have educational options and referral resources *at hand.* Specific suggestions of what parents can do at home to reinforce their child's success at school are often valued and can strengthen gains made in the school setting.

Establishing Rapport

As in any counseling situation, establishing rapport is vital. In order to build trust with parents, school professionals should be open and welcoming while giving opportunities for parents to share their extensive knowledge of their own child. From a solution-focused perspective, parents are the experts at knowing what works with their child and what the child can be encouraged to "do more of" (De Jong & Berg, 2002, p. 150). Parents are also the ones who are most likely to know and report those exceptional times when problematic behavior could have occurred but did not. Imagine the positive impact of encouraging parents to share those moments!

Presenting Information Clearly and Honestly

School-related information should be presented honestly and kindly, and, if possible, without using any kind of professional jargon. For example, since many parents do not know what standard scores are, a counselor might explain how their child did on the assessments in plain language such as, "Renee has wonderful strengths in music and math! She does as well as or better than half the children her age. It looks like the areas that we'll want to focus on are reading comprehension and social skills. In these areas, 80 percent of children her age do better than Renee, and with support, she can improve."

Although the school psychologist may be the one who explains testing scores, counselors are frequently asked questions about these issues in later meetings or encounters with parents and should be able to explain the assessments that were used and the overall test results. Counselors can also offer to discuss the results again with the psychologist.

Making Yourself Available

Remind parents that you will be there as an ongoing resource and that they can call with questions at any time. Parents often find IEP meetings overwhelming and discouraging, and will greatly appreciate being able to call later to get clarification about questions that occur to them once the meeting is over. In fact, counselors should plan to initiate such calls instead of just saying, "Call any time," or "My door is always open." Periodic contact with parents to ask how things are going with their child, what they have noticed, what is working, and similar questions will help build an effective alliance with the family. Contacting parents when something goes *right* is really appreciated. ("I noticed today that Amy sat still and was quiet during assembly. She seemed to enjoy the presentation by the veterinarian. I wonder if she'd like some books on working with animals?")

Sharing Resources

Counselors can be the crucial link for parents to exciting sources of information and support, such as family resource centers. However, this link must reflect active outreach initiatives by school counselors. The Autism Society of Southeastern Wisconsin (www.assew.org) developed a wonderful resource directory that became widely used and appreciated by families and school personnel. But several parents in more than one school district report that counselors do not share this information unless it is specifically requested. Counselors may have good intentions when they steer a family to a certain favorite provider, but families deserve access to complete information so that they can make their own choices. Parents may not know what is available, or, in some cases, may not want the school to know that they are seeking help.

Other anecdotal evidence suggests that counselors can, wittingly or unwittingly, interfere with access to donated books and materials by placing them in their own offices or even the teachers' lounge. Again, well-intended efforts to have materials on hand are sabotaged by having them available to parents only during school hours and never on weekends, holidays, or summer months. It is obvious that good intentions do not always deliver good results, which is why a systematic plan to deliver or share information is so important.

With Internet access so widely available, resource lists can be posted online. If a counselor has a private list, it can be added to a parent page on the school Web site with a resource link or links to other agencies, such as the Developmental Disabilities Council, Children and Adults with Attention-Deficit/Hyperactivity Disorder (CHADD), National Alliance for the Mentally Ill (NAMI), and so forth. Providing links to both the ASCA and the American Mental Health Counselors Association (AMHCA) Web sites is also a good idea.

Counselors can provide help by selecting a service provider when asked, but parents who are uncomfortable asking would then still have access to relevant resources. Counselors must use their best judgment, as well as professional discretion, in balancing their interests in becoming involved with the student and family with the family's right to privacy and information.

Surveying the Counseling Services

In this delicate "dance" with parents, feedback forms can let parents express their level of satisfaction with counseling services. Surveys of parent opinions can help prioritize uses of resources. Counselors can use e-mail and voice mail to communicate with many parents. (Important: remember the Health Insurance Portability and Accountability Act restrictions on transmitting confidential material!) However school counselors do it, establishing a reliable communication system is vital and will increase parental involvement and result in better services to students.

Giving Parents Active Roles

Parents can be encouraged to pursue active roles in several ways. Harry (1992) has written that parents are the first assessors of their children with disabilities. When the family has a different language, or even dialect, from the school professionals, parents become "translators" for their children's needs. Parents can and should present reports at meetings, just as other participants do. Parents can also have input on policy making at the local level and beyond. They are obvious advocates and sources of support for each other. Some parents will become leaders of advocacy organizations and many will develop expert knowledge regarding their child's disability. A few may even be interested in being part of research studies. All of these roles build family involvement as well as deserved recognition of parental competence.

Counselors often lead parent education groups, but again, the needs of parents of children with disabilities can be unique. Often, families are involved in planning and implementing behavior modification programs for their children. Counselors can be key in teaching parents to select and use appropriate techniques, such as the following:

- Consistent consequences
- Clear directions
- Parent-child play or projects
- Relationship building
- Time-outs
- Behavior extinction
- Positive communication skills

- Other cognitive behavioral techniques, such as the "stop, think, and plan" method of helping children with disabilities solve their own problems

Counselors can model positive communication for families, teach the family new ways of interacting, and provide helpful feedback. Counselors can also help parents focus on their child's strengths rather than their deficiencies; remember that parents can also help school counselors in exactly the same ways.

ADAPTING YOUR STYLE

How would your style change if you incorporated more of a systems perspective like the one briefly described in this chapter? How could you integrate this perspective with your own theory and practice of counseling? For example, if you are an Adlerian counselor, family is already an important part of the way you work with students (Halbur & Halbur, 2006). Whereas you might routinely conceptualize your students' behavior as a way to overcome feelings of inferiority and attain superiority by looking at such things as birth order and family constellation, what might it add to your work to include, for example, a genogram? Would it help all family members to realize their importance and their unique roles? Might you discover positive characteristics about the child with disabilities that you otherwise would not have learned?

The Solution-Focused Approach

School counselors who may be looking for a model to use with families are encouraged to examine Solution-Focused Brief Family Therapy (De Jong & Berg, 2002). In situations where the school counselor may not have more than four to six sessions available to work with a family, this approach is recommended. Solution-focused counselors emphasize competencies and solutions. For example, one family may bring in extended family members to help with a specific problem, whereas another family will set aside time to discuss problematic issues and resolve them in a structured way that involves only the parent(s) and the affected child. Building on "things that work" is important in working with families. Although time is in short supply for school counselors, there is ample evidence that even short-term work with families has a positive impact (Vanderbleek, 2004). Peter De Jong and Insoo Kim Berg's excellent second edition of *Interviewing for Solutions* (2002) is highly recommended.

> A school counselor may not have more than four to six sessions available to work with a student and his or her family.

Another technique that school counselors can try involves framing issues with children in terms of a family perspective. This framing can set the stage for referral to a family counselor, if necessary, and the school counselor can remain part of the system that continues to work with the family as appropriate.

Family History Approach

Regardless of your approach to counseling, consider asking a parent to work with you on a genogram (see Table 6.1 and Figure 6.1). This exercise not only empowers the parent and allows him or her to be the expert, but also produces very useful information. One parent of an autistic child was astonished to discover, by using this exercise, that most members of her husband's family had significant neurological disorders. It helped her to realize that her odds of having a child with autism were greater than they were for most people. It also helped her understand one reason why her husband's family was slow to acknowledge or accept her son's disability: they were a high-functioning family who were accustomed to unusual behavior and patterns of development in early childhood and did not see either as abnormal.

REASONS PARENTS REACT DIFFERENTLY

Creating effective partnerships with families of children with disabilities requires knowledge of their special issues. Seligman's classic and moving work, *Strategies for Helping Parents of Exceptional Children* (1979), describes the stages of grief that parents of a child with a disability may go through. Denial often comes first, followed by a bargaining stage. ("If we can just work

Table 6.1 Genogram of the Pseudo-Family of a Student With a Disability

Place in Family	Genetic Influence	Family Influence	Cultural Influence
1. Oldest child and son. Recently identified as having a learning disability in reading comprehension. Frequently reprimanded for poor attitude and work ethic at school.	Inherited genetic predisposition for a specific learning disability.	Moderate paternal pressure to succeed in school due to father's own difficulties. Mother sometimes over-protects from school consequences.	Child is first generation immigrant. Is fluent in oral English and has helped his family adjust to life in the United States. Is interested in popular American culture also values his role as eldest son.
2. Father. Successful store manager who had difficulty at school and continues to dislike the educational system, especially in the United States. Was not identified with a learning disability, but struggles with reading.	Inherited genetic predisposition for a specific learning disability.	Feels strongly about supporting dependents economically and is very family oriented. Parents did not value formal education.	Proud Mexican American identity; moved to the United States for economic reasons; very strong work ethic.
3. Mother. Works as a nurse's aide at local hospital. Academic success came easily to her. Frequently has difficulty balancing work and family identities. Would like to obtain education to become RN; this goal not supported by husband.	No genetic link to learning disability.	Her siblings' deaths had significant impact. Feels high level of responsibility to maintain family relationships with both her family of origin and creation.	Also from a traditional Mexican family. Is more assimilated to U.S. culture than her husband, but maintains pride in her own traditions and heritage.
4. Siblings. Younger sister experiences easy academic success. Younger brother receives high praise for his "good attitude" in school.	No learning challenges evident.	All three children have close emotional bonds but frequently fight over authority issues (who is in charge) in part due to the oldest son's problems in school.	Siblings are aware of their cultural heritage but are mostly differentiated and highly identify with U.S. popular culture.
5. Family of father. Close bond among youngest three siblings and parents. Oldest son was alienated from family. Father recently died.	Father and middle sons inherited genetic learning disability predisposition but none identified.	Agricultural family. Father involved in farm work and mother was homemaker. Low value on academics, other than work-oriented education learning disability. Little communication about father's death.	Strong traditional Mexican and Catholic cultural influences. High value on fairly rigid gender roles. Children not encouraged to pursue education after high school.
6. Family of mother. Lived in small city for most of family's life. Father was a factory supervisor; mother was encouraged to get an education and worked as an elementary teacher.	No genetic link to learning disability.	Emotionally close family until death of two children as teenagers in car accident. Parents have since become distant and youngest son has become an alcoholic.	Another traditional Mexican family, but more oriented to education. This family is interested in other cultures and other ways of living.

84

Figure 6.1   Genogram of the Psuedo-Family Described in Table 6.1

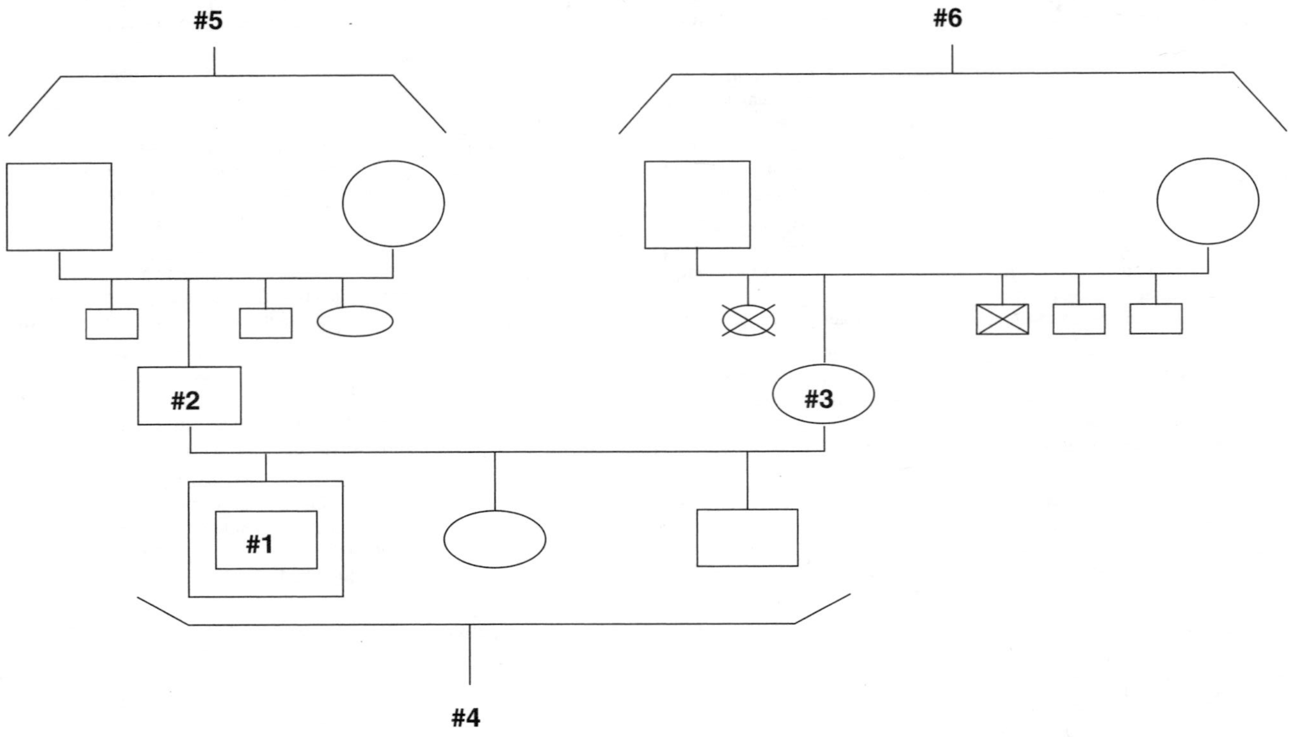

really hard with my child, things will get much better.") When full awareness of the situation is reached, parents may experience anger, guilt, and depression.

Counselors can help with these feelings in several ways, such as referring parents to family therapists and directing families to support groups and Internet-based resources. Counselors should also remember that these stages of grief might reappear as the child develops. New awareness of their child's differences or future challenges can reawaken the grief process, and counselors must be most sensitive to this pain.

Some parents may feel anger or ambivalence toward their child with a disability. Cycles of optimism and pessimism also are not uncommon. Factors such as socioeconomic status, the physical appearance of the child, prior understanding of the disability, religious or spiritual resources, and social support can greatly affect families living with a child with a disability.

Differing Responses of Mothers and Fathers

In looking at patterns among families of children with disabilities, it has been noted in the literature and in the authors' experience that mothers of children with learning disabilities can be overprotective, overinvolved, and even enmeshed. Fathers of these children, on the other hand, can be distant, sometimes to the point of disengagement or denial of the disability or disabling condition. These two reactions reinforce each other, for as fathers establish a distance comfortable to them, mothers feel a need to become even more actively engaged in meeting their child's needs. Marital break-ups are not uncommon. If both parents are willing to participate in counseling sessions, they might see the dynamics of the situation more clearly and be able to better support each other and their child.

Two Common Questions

The depth and range of parents' feelings about their children with disabilities may be affected by two elements, reflected in the questions "Is the disability acquired or congenital?" and "What is the severity of the disability?"

For example, parents of students with disabilities acquired through accident or disease sometimes show overall difficulty in adjusting to the new realities their child faces. This lack of adjustment is because the family is adapting to the child becoming a person who now has a disability.

In contrast, parents of children with congenital disabilities often have trouble achieving emotional distance from their child, due in part to the chronic sorrow of the situation. In either of these two cases, the greater the severity of the disability, the more impact there will be on the family, its functioning, and its future.

> If families first learn of an identified disability from the school, counselors can be alerted to offer assistance and support, and to handle communication in the most direct yet gentle manner.

Reasons for the disability (heredity versus accident, for example) and how parents found out about it can also influence the ways parents view the child and the situation as a whole. Because of sonograms, amniocentesis techniques, and increasing understanding of human genetics, some families will find out before their child is born that he or she has a genetically linked disability. This knowledge can prepare families in many ways to love and care for the coming child.

However, being called by the school and told in a cold, clinical way that your six-year-old son has a severe learning disability is another experience entirely. Suddenly finding out that a child has a disability almost always precipitates a family crisis. If families first learn of an identified disability from the school, counselors can be alerted to offer assistance and support, and to handle communication in the most direct yet gentle manner.

Often it is hard to tell from the outside what level of emotional distance is appropriate among parents and children with disabilities. Because of differences between the child's developmental or emotional level and his or her chronological age, for example, parents may relate to the child in what looks like an odd or out-of-step manner. Counselors are reminded that parents of children with disabilities are used to constantly mediating between their children and the world. What might appear to be over-involvement may really be the best way to help that child cope. Remember that parents are the experts in what works with their child! Also keep in mind that parents are individuals; their actions and feelings can vary widely from one another (Gargiulo, 2004).

Parenting Styles

Parenting styles will be different, depending on the needs of the individual child. Mothers and fathers have usually worked hard to discover how to help their children succeed. On the other hand, some parents can become discouraged and overwhelmed by their child's needs. School counselors can act as bridges between families and the educational community as well as families and other resources for children with disabilities. Counselors are accustomed to referring families to agencies in the community, but must familiarize themselves with organizations such as United Cerebral Palsy, the Autism Society of America, Learning Disabilities Association of America, Children with Attention Deficit Disorders, and the like, when working with students who have disabilities. Most of these groups have local or state chapters that are extremely helpful to parents. Web sites allow parents to network all over the world with people who know a great deal about specific disabilities and treatments as well as school-based interventions (see Resource A).

Counselors can mediate the sometimes-volatile feelings that arise in parents raising a child with certain disabilities, as well as the strong feelings of teachers who are struggling with classroom management and the needs of groups of children. These mediation skills are invaluable in situations that often pair insecure teachers ("I don't know how to teach your child!") with frustrated parents ("Why do you have that job, then?").

These situations, although inherently unfair to all involved, occur frequently in schools. Teachers often resent the perceived interference, lack training, are afraid of failing, or are apprehensive about how much time and energy students with disabilities may take away from their efforts to work with the rest of the class. Counselors can point out that adversarial relationships among the adults (in addition to being largely unpleasant) hurt the children, while collaborative efforts are more productive for all involved, most of all the children.

IEP meetings can be ideal opportunities for sharing new information regarding the student and can help change the systems (both at school and at home) in which the child lives. Decisions based solely on educational information, for any child, without consideration of family circumstances, may in fact be harmful to the student.

Within the school, counselors can also point out to teachers the extensive evidence that teaching techniques useful for students in special education may enhance the learning of all students. Similarly, counselors may need to remind themselves that the family inclusion model discussed in this chapter is a helpful model for working with all children.

Shifted Expectations of Life Development

Another factor that affects how a family reacts to a child with a disability is the stage of family life development in which it happens to be. Although there are anticipated stages of family life and development, families with children who have disabilities may not experience all of these stages, or may experience them differently and at times different from other families. One major family transition is when children leave home. Most counselors (and parents) will see right away that for many families of children with disabilities the children may not leave home on time or possibly ever. So, as you examine family systems theory and consider approaches to apply to your own counseling, be sure to be sensitive to ways in which your approaches might need to be adapted for use with families that might not follow the typical patterns or stages of family life and development.

Remember that family stages are associated with developmental tasks. How the family experiences and negotiates these stages and tasks will affect how it faces and works through subsequent stages and tasks. For instance, it is the family's job to successfully socialize young children into the larger community, which includes school. How the family has done this in the past affects how it expects to do this in the future. If a family's first child is a child with a disability that impairs functioning in school, that experience may color the expectations those parents have when subsequently bringing to school their children who do not have disabilities. Counselors will find it helpful to recall that complex processes of this nature will influence not only families, but also how the families are viewed by school personnel.

SEXUALITY

Sexuality is another area in which parents will react differently, both within a specific family and among families at large. The range of values and the somewhat inherent emotionality of this issue can be complicated by the effects of disabilities. School counselors can be extremely helpful to parents dealing with the sexual behavior of their child with a disability. They may assist parents in determining what and how to teach the child about sexuality. Counselors can model how to deal with this issue in a straightforward, sensible, and empathetic way.

Parents of children with disabilities may have trouble seeing their offspring as sexual beings. The online journal *Disability Solutions* (www.disabilitysolutions.org) offers resources on many topics, including healthy attitudes toward sexuality for people with disabilities. The issue on sexuality education notes that the more severe the disability, the less likely parents feel the need to address sexuality issues with their children.

Family Values

It is important to respect both the family's values and the directives of the school district in this area. For example, one school counselor believed it would be better to advise a young man with autism and moderate cognitive delays to masturbate in the privacy of his bedroom rather than in the classroom. The family strongly disagreed, and a huge conflict developed. They believed the counselor's job was to teach their son that all masturbation is wrong. Parents are, rightly, the primary providers of sex-related information for their children. However, peers, television and movies, print materials, places of worship, and life experiences are additional sources of information. Sometimes students with disabilities have fewer opportunities to learn about sexuality than other students do. As these students mature, they may have trouble making sex-related decisions; they may also be at greater risk of exploitation.

A Blurring of Public and Private

Terri Couwenhoven, mother of a child with Down syndrome, points out that children and youth with certain disabilities may not have the information or understanding to deal well with sexual situations for several reasons. These include, but are not limited to, the fact that some students with disabilities depend on others to assist them with daily living needs; they may learn to be compliant with authority figures; they may lack social skills or advanced reasoning ability; and they are exposed to several caregivers (Couwenhoven, 2001).

Privacy for people with developmental disabilities is not always respected. It can be quite a challenge for those who grow up desensitized to notions of privacy to learn to distinguish between public and private behavior. Obviously, these risk factors vary with the nature and severity of the disability, but all increase the vulnerability of children with disabilities and underscore the need for appropriate education about sexuality.

Although all humans are sexual beings, people with disabilities are often viewed as asexual. And sometimes those who are overtly sexual are seen as monsters or people who have no self-control. School counselors working in this area may need to use advocacy; interventions; education; and support with parents, other students, and even the public.

Puberty

Puberty is usually a time of great stress for parents of a child with disabilities. Of course, this is a time of anxiety for parents of all children, but for parents of children with disabilities it is even more complex. Sexual development can occur as it does typically, which results in one set of challenges, but it can also be complicated by certain disabilities. For example, some students identified with an emotional or behavior disorder may express sexuality by exposing themselves in the classroom, which is clearly not acceptable behavior.

School counselors can provide resources or programs in a variety of areas, such as how to talk with children about sexuality, birth control, homosexuality, and masturbation; how to protect themselves from sexual predators; and how to make wise decisions. Counselors can search for "materials specifically designed for people with disabilities, design alternative teaching techniques for addressing sexual issues, help families identify resources within the community, and supplement and reinforce sexuality concepts" as appropriate (Couwenhoven, 2001, p. 5). Young people with disabilities need to be able to have healthy self-esteem, good body image, and opportunities to socialize appropriately (Fine, 1991).

WORKING WITH THE SIBLINGS
OF CHILDREN WITH DISABILITIES

Another way to build partnerships with families is to work with the brothers and sisters of children who have disabilities. Siblings of children with disabilities often benefit greatly from attention from the school counselor. This group, even though it is at risk for developing problems, is frequently ignored. Sometimes called "shadow siblings," children who grow up with brothers or sisters who have a disability can bear some burdens, but can also be greatly enriched by the experience (Robertson, 2006).

From fielding rude questions (e.g., "What's the matter with Ben? He looks weird!") to gaining maturity and compassion at an early age, siblings have unique challenges but also blessings and opportunities to learn. They can become their sister's strongest defender or pretend in school that their brother does not exist. For parents, this can cause pride and, alternatively, sadness, sometimes on the same day! Within the family, the needs of the child with a disability can sometimes overshadow the needs of other children.

Girls, especially eldest daughters, are likely to be most affected by having a sibling with a disability. They are often relied upon to provide extra nurturing or to assume other adult responsibilities, making them feel that they have grown up too fast. On the positive side, the sibling of a child with a disability can learn empathy and feel needed in the family. On the negative side, the children who do not have a disability sometimes have unrealistic expectations put on them in order to compensate for the challenges of the sibling with a disability.

Group Counseling With Siblings

School counselors are well equipped to provide group experiences for children who have brothers or sisters with disabilities. Learning and sharing information about disabilities is a good group activity. Children usually have many unanswered questions about what causes disabilities. They wonder if the disability is contagious ("Will I become deaf, too?"). They wonder if the disability will ever go away ("Will my sister ever be like other kids?"). Discussing feelings and attitudes toward siblings or parents is also helpful. Finding out that their family has common ground with other families and is also unique is comforting to children. Finally, role-playing can help children better understand a parent's role, or even the constraints on the sister or brother with a disability. Some siblings of children with disabilities can become advocates for students with disabilities in the school, whereas others have no desire to be singled out in this manner. Obviously, assumptions cannot be made, and parents and students need to be consulted before counselors select any of these options.

In Minnesota, the previously mentioned PACER (Parent Advocacy Coalition for Educational Rights) Center offers resources to families of children with special needs (www.pacer .org), including social inclusion fun nights of bowling, movies, or tours. And in many locales, "Sibshops" provide support, education, and activities for siblings of children with disabilities (Meyer & Vadasy, 1994).

Slade (1988) pointed out that school counselors should pay attention to four elements in particular when working with the siblings of children with disabilities. These include parental attitudes toward the child with a disability, the gender and birth order of the sibling who does not have a disability, the type and severity of the problems affecting the child with disabilities, and the parenting style experienced by the sibling without disabilities. Siblings of children with disabilities can exhibit many adjustment issues, including academic performance difficulties and behavioral concerns. School counselors should be alert to these concerns and help families deal with them.

FAMILY DIVERSITY

Most school counselors are well educated with regard to diversity issues, and will certainly notice cultural differences among families. However, when the counselor comes from an ethnic or cultural background different than the family, offensive assumptions on both sides are often still made. People from many cultures are extremely reluctant to discuss family issues with a counselor who does not have first-hand knowledge of their experience. Excellent resources are available to help counselors learn how to work effectively with people from varying cultural and ethnic backgrounds (see Suggested Readings).

As noted, minority students and students from economically disadvantaged backgrounds are more frequently identified as having learning disabilities in particular. Overidentification puts these students at risk of not reaching their academic potential, and is likely to affect them socially and emotionally as well (Gargiulo, 2005). Some educators believe that children with disabilities constitute a culturally different group themselves, simply due to the impact of their disabilities. When students with disabilities and their families are also members of a racial or cultural minority group, or are poor, they may suffer several kinds of discrimination, even oppression. Being informed and aware of these issues can bring school counselors from an unhelpful "I feel sorry for you" position to a more unbiased perspective that acknowledges the complexities and realities faced by these families.

In working with families of various cultures, counselors can relate in ways that allow cultural identity to be a strength (through kinship networks, traditions, and heritage), as well as honor family values. In any case, matching the best techniques to the child and the unique family situation is vital.

> In working with families of various cultures, counselors can relate in ways that allow cultural identity to be a strength (through kinship networks, traditions, and heritage), as well as honor family values.

Although many counselors like to think that "all children are children," and this is correct to some extent, there are historical dimensions to working with families of color or families in poverty that cannot be ignored. African American parents, for example, report that they often perceive that school personnel make negative assumptions about their families' ability to participate in school-sponsored groups in positive ways. Counselors need to ask themselves whether they see parent education as an opportunity for dialogue or a chance to show parents how things are supposed to be done. A deficit model that views parent education as addressing weaknesses will not be effective, and is not an ethical approach.

Be Mindful of Your Own Assumptions

Sometimes, multicultural education serves only to reinforce stereotypes or to oversimplify individual and family situations. Assumptions (e.g., a family from a certain culture will be more or less likely to accept professional interventions) will be rightly challenged if counselors listen carefully, learn a specific family's values, and work in supportive, nonjudgmental ways (Turnbull, Turnbull, Erwin, & Soodak, 2006). So-called norms are contradicted by everyday practice in most schools. Economically disadvantaged families often suffer from assumptions made about them. These families may also bring differing realities with them, such as lack of a phone, Internet access, transportation, or available time (due to working several jobs, etc.). It can take more time and creativity for school counselors to develop trust with parents in these circumstances and to engage those parents as partners in their children's education.

Some parents of students with disabilities have disabilities themselves. These may exacerbate the logistical challenges present with most families, such as transportation and scheduling. Situations like these require perhaps the most flexibility and sensitivity on the part of school counselors, who should work toward joint decision making, even when the parents have developmental disabilities.

Many times counselors are tempted to view nontraditional families as having problems before really getting to know if that is the case. Some single-parent families, for example, are very strong and have a multitude of sources of support. That stated, however, it is important to watch for the possible impact of financial constraints, emotional overload, and family management issues, especially in families having children with disabilities. With fewer adults to carry responsibility in the family, money and emotional energy may be in short supply. With all families, and nontraditional families in particular, counselors must be open to very flexible scheduling of appointments and should also consider visiting the family home (with permission). Even experienced counselors can mistake difficulty in getting together with lack of parental interest or commitment.

Working With Stepfamilies

Stepfamilies have distinct issues as well. All stepfamilies have their origins in loss of some type. Disruption of attachment is almost always present. Stepfamilies often begin with unrealistically high expectations. With no shared history of child rearing, a lack of clear roles in the family, and few, if any, existing patterns or rituals to help them, stepfamilies are challenged in many ways. Counselors can be very helpful in clarifying roles and boundaries. They can also work with children in stepfamilies to encourage the creation of new traditions or rituals that support family stability.

When a stepfamily has a child with disabilities, stresses usually increase. School personnel need to remember that stepparents, for legal reasons, often cannot make emergency medical decisions involving a stepchild. Stepparents may really struggle as they discover what it is like to have daily parental responsibility for a child with a disability.

Working With Adoptive and Foster Parents

Adoptive parents have varying concerns as well, often linked to the age of the child when adopted. The child, if older, may have separation or attachment anxieties or disorders. If there are other children in the family, loyalty conflicts may emerge, especially if the adopted child has disabilities. There may be questions or even judgments about how the disability was acquired (e.g., fetal alcohol syndrome).

Foster parents are often even less empowered. Their interaction with schools usually includes a social worker. Foster parents must have permission from this person for most school-based interventions.

Working With Nontraditional Families

Nontraditional families are now the majority in American society. Counselors need to remember that insurance issues, confidentiality, legal liability, and family tensions may be very complicated in some families. Counselors must keep in mind that all of these families want to function successfully as family units and take good care of their children. Each family and its set of circumstances are unique, however, and counselors are required to show sensitivity, respect, and professionalism in all cases. This is especially challenging when parents and counselors have different values (e.g., toward cohabiting parents, or gay or lesbian parents). If counselors consistently present themselves as positive resources to families and recognize that these families want the best for their children, much can be accomplished.

CONCLUDING COMMENTS

It is important for counselors to help others remember to not focus solely on the disability of an individual child, but to look to the larger context, including family dynamics, the school situation, and even the community setting. The systems perspective, with which most counselors are familiar, lends a more universal and encompassing view.

Family systems counseling is emerging as an effective way to conceptualize many issues. In the school setting, the student is usually seen as the identified person with a problem. This is particularly true in the case of a child who has a disability; the child is seen as the one who is involved with counseling. A systems approach may startle family members at first, who may prefer to think of that child as the one with the problem. When families can come to understand the systemic nature of many issues for children, they may be more willing to join in family therapy.

Even in cases where the child is the one with an identified concern, as is most common in situations where the school is the first to contact the parents, it is helpful and often instills hope for family members to participate in counseling. For example, families with a child who has Fragile X syndrome may be astonished at how valuable it is to experience the support of good counseling. A systems approach can help the family gain perspective on how living with a child who has a significantly challenging disability affects their marital and sibling relationships, and adds stress to many aspects of family life. With the help of the systems approach, the parents and family members of this child, in addition to the hard work of regular parenting, can be helped to draw on almost superhuman amounts of patience, creativity, resourcefulness, and optimism.

What else can school counselors do to work better with the families of children with disabilities? We all know at some cognitive level that the children we see in our schools are parts of systems that change whenever one part, or person, alone is changed or treated, but we seem to forget it in important ways and at important times. We also know that, with families, the whole is greater than the sum of its parts, but often we still focus on just that part—or child—before us. Although many counselors may not have the time or expertise to offer family therapy, we can and must make time to familiarize ourselves with the resources available for good referrals. And counselors can certainly be the available and honest communication link between school personnel and families, all of whom care about the success of children.

CHAPTER SEVEN

Making a Difference in the Wider Circle of Caring

From the beginning, this book has encouraged school counselors to take a proactive stance by inviting themselves into the world of students who bring not only their hopes, dreams, and aspirations to school, but also their disabilities.

This book has presented material on knowing the legal context for working with students who are eligible for services through IDEA and 504 legislation, working with the multidisciplinary or IEP team, employing a variety of assessment techniques and instruments, using a delivery system that employs the TREAT model, and writing effective goals. This book has also shared ideas for working with the families of students with disabilities who school counselors will serve.

It is a lot to keep in mind! However, the theme of *this* chapter is that professional school counselors serve all students well by simply (simply!) being *good school counselors*. Time-limited individual counseling is an option for counselors to assist a certain number of students who have been identified as needing counseling services. The vast majority of students, including those with disabilities, however, are well served by large- and small-group interventions, which counselors already do each day. This perspective "switches the counselor's emphasis from being service-centered for some students to being program-centered for every student" (ASCA, 2004, p.1).

Successful counseling programs and those who manage them suggest that counselors ask the question "How are students different because of what we (school counselors) do?" (ASCA, 2004, p. 1). In this age of No Child Left Behind and overall increased accountability, how can school counselors demonstrate that we are making a difference? And how can we intensify our efforts in ways that improve our effectiveness? Results-based efforts begin with the end (or outcome) in mind. How do counselors keep optimal outcomes in mind as we make decisions about how to expend our limited time, energy, and resources? And how do we best address the needs of students with disabilities within this perspective?

One way to approach these questions is to use the guidance and expertise available through the American School Counselor Association (ASCA). The assumptions or principles upon which the national model for school counseling programs rests include (a) leadership, (b) advocacy, (c) collaboration, and (d) systemic change. The model, available on the ASCA Web site, is conceptually broad and promotes student growth in personal and social development, career planning, and academic success. When developed and managed correctly, school counseling functions will connect directly to the mission of the school and, thereby, to all students, including those with disabilities.

LEADERSHIP

As part of the educational leadership team in a school, counselors can share their substantial expertise. School counselors are the resident behavior and relationship experts who are charged with helping all students reach their maximum potential. They are also leaders, change agents, advocates, and collaborators for the students in their schools. School counselors help students make sense of their thoughts, feelings, and behaviors in order to set and reach their academic and personal development goals. This clearly is in line with any school's mission.

Counselors bring to the leadership table advanced education and skills in behavior management, child development, individual and group counseling, assessment, school-to-work transitions, and more. This expertise is intended for all students, and students with disabilities have a legal right to the benefits of the school's comprehensive guidance program. In fact, what school counselors do must be seen as an integral part of the overall academic mission of the school. The principle of leadership is of particular importance when it comes to children with unique learning needs. Helping students learn will require more intervention in some cases than in others. Counseling is but one form of intervention. Although classroom guidance activities support the learning process, some students may need small group or individual support as well. Psycho-educational groups and classroom guidance activities that focus on such skills as studying, organizing, and test taking may be of particular value to students with certain disabilities.

An organized and well-planned guidance curriculum is vital. As in any other curricular area, guidance should be categorized around specific topics. These topics usually include career development, self-management, motivation, self-esteem, and other social-emotional and life-skills areas. The school counselor can demonstrate leadership in these areas, and in others, by having strong curriculum units that address each topic. These units should include appropriate modifications to make the material accessible to all students. An appropriate modification might involve having an interpreter present for the child with a hearing impairment during a lesson on helping first graders cope with fears that include reading a story aloud in class. Guidance activities often incorporate class discussion. If there is a student who is mute or has an expressive language disorder, one option is to provide assistive technology that the student can use in order to participate. Teachers and counselors repeatedly report that these types of alternatives help not only students with disabilities but also enhance the learning of other students in the group.

ADVOCACY

Counselors are in a unique and vital position to act as advocates for students who are eligible for special education services. The ASCA position statement on students with special needs (adopted 1999; revised 2004) says, "Professional school counselors advocate for all students and provide collaborative services to students with special needs consistent with those services provided to students through the comprehensive school counseling program" (see Resource B).

Advocacy is a key school counselor responsibility. Being an advocate includes supporting, creating, and carrying out program accommodations and modifications at school and sometimes also within the community. Advocacy also involves helping students learn to become advocates for themselves.

Early Identification

One form of advocacy is *early identification*. Increasingly, school counselors are called upon to assess young children who may have developmental delays or complications. Many schools invite their school counselor to participate in "kindergarten round-up." Assessment can involve asking key questions, such as the following:

- How well does Matthew play with others?
- Does Callie share her toys?
- What does Jesse do when he is told no?
- Does Carter like to pretend when he plays?

Early intervention is seen to have the highest impact, making early identification of possible disabilities increasingly important.

Creative Programs

Being an advocate can mean sponsoring creative programs, such as the circle of friends networks or friendship groups for students with or without disabilities. Other buddy programs assign a student with or without disabilities to assist a student with disabilities in a certain task or activity, such as hanging out at recess or tutoring in reading. Students with disabilities are often totally excluded from extracurricular activities other than those designed especially for them, such as the Special Olympics. Some parents report that they must be assertive in getting permission for their children to participate in extracurricular activities. In addition, parents of children with disabilities often are required to bend their schedules in ways other parents do not in order to accommodate scheduling and transportation needs. In fact, many parents of children with disabilities must become the coach or activity leader if they want their child to be included.

Counselors can advocate for these students and parents within the school setting and commit the school to increasing access to activities for all students. Counselors willing to serve as catalysts for these kinds of changes in the school and community provide immense help to students with disabilities.

Connecting Families With Resources

School counselors speak for children who sometimes have no voice and no power at school or sometimes even at home. Advocacy overlaps to a great extent with an issue presented later—collaboration—in that it often involves connecting students and parents with existing services and programs, such as well-established advocacy organizations (see Resource A). Many families that have children with autism may not know of the outstanding network of information and support offered by the Autism Society of America and its state and local chapters. In this day of electronic communication, a family's best ally may prove to be a parent living thousands of miles away who can share crucial information.

Small-Group Guidance

Advocacy is not just doing *for;* it is doing *with,* and teaching *how.* Developmental guidance is well suited to help students with disabilities enhance their self-acceptance, self-understanding, and ability to self-advocate. These traits may be best modeled and promoted in small groups of students with similar disabilities and through classroom guidance.

For example, students with specific learning disabilities comprise the largest and fastest-growing segment of children with disabilities. Forming groups of four to six students who have been identified as having learning disabilities can offer group members the opportunity to see what makes them unique as learners, as well as what they may have in common. In a small group, students may share coping techniques and other resources and may learn how to ask for what they need in the classroom. These students may come to recognize and value what they bring to the school. Groups give students a sense of safety, belonging, and a place to practice fledgling skills that will benefit them in the classroom, lunchroom, bandroom, or playground. We encourage counselors to facilitate groups, gather data on student response, and determine how students with learning disabilities improve in the classroom as a result. (See Webb & Myrick, 2003, which presents a fully developed group unit designed for students with ADHD.)

Access to School Activities

Counselors are in positions to observe marginalized groups and to encourage broad access to, and participation in, school activities.

Along with their other essential duties, counselors are in the business of instilling hope. Some students with disabilities carry a sense of discouragement every day! They are aware of their differences at a time of life when fitting in and being like everyone else is most prized. Students who use wheelchairs know that they will never play baseball like Derek Jeter. But is there a wheelchair baseball team at your school, and if not, could one be started? Students with severe reading disabilities are often convinced that they are stupid. Do they know that Jay Leno, Whoopi Goldberg, Tom Cruise, and Orlando Bloom function *very* well despite that disability? Are the students with disabilities encouraged to develop a talent that they can share in the school talent show?

Counselors should be as concerned with helping students maximize their potential as they are with a test result or diagnosis. Always acknowledge accomplishments with comments like, "Jerome is sight impaired; he reads very well in braille and is a superb guitar player." It is really important to keep the focus on abilities rather than disabilities. Counselors can link student interests to opportunities within and beyond the school to develop those interests and aptitudes.

The following true story, although it does not involve a counselor, is a great illustration of what a kind and sincere gesture can accomplish (identifying information has been altered):

Nick Hudson is a high school senior living in Omaha, Nebraska. Nick is a very bright and engaging young man, with strong computer skills and a gift for singing. Nick has an autism spectrum disorder; he has a history of outbursts when things do not go his way, and has a hard time handling disappointment. Nick is a huge fan of many sports teams, including his school's basketball teams. Because of Nick's great interest in basketball, the coaches of both the boys' and girls' teams took an interest in him. In his senior year, Nick attended every game, including away games. The girls' team advanced to the playoffs, but lost the championship game in a heartbreaker. Nick's heart, too, was broken, and he was embarrassed after he broke down and cried in front of other students. He was so upset that he could not face going to school the next day. Nick's mom received the following e-mail from the counselor containing the message that had been read to all students over the intercom at school:

Thank you to all of the students and staff who came out to support the girls' basketball team Saturday night. While the results were not what we had hoped for, we are all proud to represent East High and will continue to work hard to make East proud of us. The entire team and coaching staff would also like to give special recognition to our super-fan, Nick Hudson. Your support means a lot to us, and anybody who is willing to travel to all of our away games is a great friend and a great fan. You have truly earned the title "Number 1 Super-Fan." You rock, Nick!!!

The impact of this kind of affirmation is priceless. What can you do at your school to recognize and show appreciation for the contributions that students bring? Are the contributions of students who have disabilities shared, too, widely and often? This is another aspect of advocacy. Finally, school counselors realize that the need for advocacy for students with disabilities does not end when the student graduates. Helping families and students with disabilities to become effective advocates for themselves is essential.

COLLABORATION AND TEAMING

Being an active, effective member of multidisciplinary teams that work with students on IEPs can be one way school counselors are involved in regular collaboration. Counselors *must* be directly involved in designing and writing IEP goals that relate to the services that they provide. Counselors often collaborate with others in the delivery of services, and should be committed to deliver only those services that call upon counseling expertise. Collaboration occurs in school, in the community, and in the wider world. Appropriate referrals are another way to actively collaborate, and most counselors do referrals every day.

Working With Teachers

The majority of teachers want to work collaboratively with school counselors. They care a great deal about their students, but it can be hard for them to pinpoint social or behavioral concerns during a typical one-hour class. Counselors in any school situation may be asked to come up with suggestions, such as active learning techniques or ideas for cooperative learning groups, in order to help students succeed. Counselors are also likely to be consulted to create behavioral management plans for students who bring disruptive or unproductive conduct to the classroom.

Designing Transition Plans

School counselors have a clear and vital role in helping all students plan transitions from grade to grade, from school to school, and from school to the postschool world. For students with special needs, transition planning begins before or at age fourteen. Counselors help students create and carry out goals for the future and work with families in establishing those goals. School counselors actively network with interested parties and outside resources, and share information readily and in several formats.

College advisors tell us that they often receive old, outdated information from students' high schools. Sometimes a student has not been evaluated since the eighth grade, making it difficult to know exactly when and where to place that student in the college curriculum. Establishing whether a student needs a remedial course in writing or math, or regular access to a campus counselor, needs to be based on the most current data available. Students with disabilities headed to postsecondary institutions need their school counselors to advocate for and support them in requesting up-to-date psycho-educational reports. It is critically important that students who express a sincere interest in enrolling in college get the help they need to adequately prepare for that endeavor— including up-to-date assessments and evaluations. High school counselors are in uniquely appropriate positions to provide recent evaluations and network with college transition coordinators.

As more and more students with disabilities (especially learning disabilities) now attend college, school counselors can offer extremely useful information that will help those students succeed. Of course, a well-written and current IEP is helpful, but the IEP at the college level is no longer a binding document. College accommodations fall under Section 504 of the ADA and do not include modifications, regardless of what was available to the student in high school. At the postsecondary level, most documentation must be current, revealing the specifics of the disability, as well as the status or impact of the disability in an academic setting. The evaluation must be performed by a certified or licensed professional. Appropriate college personnel will then evaluate the documentation and decide if the student qualifies as an individual with a disability and what academic adjustments are available. Ideally, the process becomes a partnership between the student and the college.

When students meet with designated advisors in postsecondary settings, the students can sign a release of information form that allows school counselors to share information that can enhance student success with college personnel. Especially in cases when the learner has been identified as LD-NOS (learning disability not otherwise specified), the school counselor can explain the student's learning challenges in ways that will increase access to assistive technology and other support services.

And while collaboration and teaming are undoubtedly central tasks for school counselors, there are limits to what counselors should take on. ASCA's position statement (see Resource B) clearly says that it is *inappropriate* for the professional school counselor to serve in "supervisory or administrative roles," such as making placement or retention decisions, supervising the implementation of IDEA, coordinating the 504 planning team, and similar activities. Counselors need to protect their time and energy to focus on activities within their purview and expertise.

Continuing Professional Education

School counselors must be committed to ongoing continuing education and professional development. This represents collaboration within the field. ASCA resources, among others, will help school counselors maintain, update, and expand their skills in making the school's comprehensive counseling programs and services appropriate for, and helpful to, all students. The American Counseling Association (ACA) and ASCA are key professional development organizations for counselors. Their national and state conferences, as well as their print and online publications, offer counselors useful information for improving their practice.

SYSTEMIC CHANGE—BEGINNING WITH YOU

Hatch and Bowers (2002) state:

> As school counselors become proficient in retrieving and analyzing school data to improve student success, they ensure educational equity for every student. Using strong communication, consultation, and political skills, school counselors

collaborate with other professionals in the school building to influence systemic change and advocate for every student. Designing a strong foundation requires effort and conviction to determine what every student will receive as a benefit of a school counseling program. (p.16)

What do you bring to your encounters with students and families? What are the assumptions you bring to your work? More specifically, what are your assumptions about students with disabilities (or maybe about those with *particular* disabilities)? As this book has noted, the most powerful element in counseling is the quality of the interpersonal relationship. What really goes into the relationships you seek to build with students, including those who have disabilities?

If language is one of the counselor's most powerful tools, what language do you use to construct student-counselor and parent-counselor relationships? Do you take time to hear each student's individual story, or are you sometimes tempted to see a diagnosis and form an opinion of what you will see, rather than *whom* you will see?

The lens you bring to each meeting focuses the interaction in specific ways. If you are looking for deficits, you will see deficits. If you are looking for strengths, you will see strengths. What do you tell *yourself* about the student with Asperger's syndrome, and how might that affect your work with him?

Decide in advance what you want your role to be with regard to students who have disabilities. How can you participate (or even show leadership!) in creating solutions rather than becoming mired down in problems? When you get into an oppositional situation with a parent, are you able to model the kind of response you would like to see if you were that parent?

Becvar and Becvar (2006) recommend the following:

- *Suspend judgment.* Assume that all behavior makes sense in context, and learn as much as possible about that context. Feel and demonstrate compassion and acceptance.
- *Be very sensitive to language.* What you call something or someone, especially with regard to a disability, is important. Reality is constructed with language, and your language has power. Choose language everyone can understand.
- *Reframe behavior in positive terms whenever possible.* Think creatively from the perspective of the student or parent.

- *Affirm your students and their families.* Acknowledge their efforts and remember that they are the experts on their own lives.
- *Work with solutions rather than problems.* Explore what is working for the family and see if family members can build on their successes.

Do you ever see your students as heroes? What about that cheerful and hard-working nine-year-old girl with a significant developmental disability who is realizing more every year that she is not like the other children in her class? What about the father who comes to meeting after meeting and speaks up for his teenage son with a social anxiety disorder? How brave must one be to face teachers and administrators who try unsuccessfully to hide the fact that they wish your child would just go away and become someone else's problem? What about the cheerleader who sustained a permanent spinal cord injury that changes everything about the future she had planned? School counselors are privileged to be daily surrounded by heroes. We also have the opportunity, almost daily, to behave heroically and literally change the world for our students, including our students with disabilities.

This final example may help you answer the following question: After reading this book, would you feel better prepared to provide and document effective interventions for this student?

A Closer Look: Donny

Donny is a student in Ms. Campbell's second-grade class. Ms. Campbell says that Donny has difficulty attending to what is going on in the classroom. He is constantly looking around, and is in and out of his chair a dozen times before morning recess. Instead of raising his hand, Donny blurts out what he hopes is the right answer to a question. Generally, his responses have nothing to do with the question asked, but rather about his favorite NASCAR driver.

With other students, Donny seems to have a habit of acting first and thinking later. For example, at lunch one day, he purposely upset the full tray of another boy. He later said, "I don't know what happened. I just saw my hand go out and tip it over." He seemed confused by the other boy's anger, and even more confused when the lunchroom supervisor tried to talk to him about it. Donny's mother says, "He can be a little hyper," and admits that he is easily overexcited and impulsive.

Does Donny have a disability? What are Donny's special needs? How can you as the counselor help him succeed in school? With the help of this book, you know that you will keep track of your personal observations of Donny as well as collect impressions, both formal and informal, from parents and teachers. You will note whether his behavior is significantly different from that of other seven-year-old boys. You will review his school records. You will talk with Donny himself about what he thinks is going on with his behavior at school.

Maybe Donny would best be helped by participating in a small group for boys his age who need to learn and practice social and impulse-control skills. Or maybe his behavior is evidence of something more serious. Your work as the school counselor will be key in obtaining an accurate assessment and creating possible interventions with this student. Your role in this situation, as in so many others, may make the difference between Donny's success and failure in school.

CONCLUDING COMMENTS

Now let's go back to the scene that opens this book. You come into the office at the end of a productive day. During this day, you have facilitated classroom guidance with the aid of an interpreter. In one of your friendship groups, you used a variety of experiential exercises to accommodate students with various disabilities. You set up parent education groups, including one for parents of children with disabilities.

And now, maybe tired and ready to go home, you see it: the IEP invitation. How do you react? Well, you might still wonder how you are going to squeeze one more thing into your busy work schedule. But now that you have studied the issues discussed in this book, you know a little more about special education law and your role in the delivery of services. As you look over the notice, you may almost automatically begin formulating a plan for how you will begin the process of knowing this student and the counseling-related concerns to be noted on the IEP. You may reflect with confidence not only about what you will bring to the team meeting, but also what you can offer to each student who comes through your door seeking help.

Resource A

Professional Organizations

AC-ACLD, Inc./An Association for Children and Adults with
  Learning Disabilities
4900 Girard Road
Pittsburg, PA 15227
(412) 881-2253
http://www.acldonline.org/aboutsld.htm

Attention Deficit Disorders Association (ADDA)
8091 South Ireland Way
Aurora, CO 80016
(800) 487-2282
http://www.add.org

Attention Deficit Disorders Association of Parents and
  Professionals Together (ADDAPPT)
P.O. Box 293
Oak Forest, IL 60452
Publishes *ADDaptibility Newsletter*

American School Counselor Association (ASCA)
1101 King Street, Suite 625
Alexandria, VA 22314
(800) 306-4722
http://www.schoolcounselor.org

Autism Society of America (ASA)
7910 Woodmont Avenue, Suite 650
Bethesda, MD 20814
(301) 657-0881
http://www.autism-society.org

Breaking the Silence
NAMI Queens/ Nassau
1983 Marcus Avenue C-103
Lake Success, NY 11042
(516) 326-0797
http://www.btslessonplans.org/

Children and Adults with Attention Deficit Disorders (CHADD)
499 NW 70th Avenue #109
Plantation, FL 33317
(305) 587-3700
http://www.chadd.org

Council for Exceptional Children (CEC)
1920 Association Drive
Reston, VA 22091
(703) 620-3660 or (703) 264-9462
http://www.cec.sped.org

Learning Disabilities Association of America (LDAA)
4156 Library Road
Pittsburgh, PA 15234
(412) 341-1515
http://www.ldanatl.org

National Association for the Education of African American
    Children with Learning Disabilities (NAEAACLD)
P.O. Box 09521
Columbus, OH 43209
(614) 237-6021
http://www.charityadvantage.com/aacld

National Center for Learning Disabilities (NCLD)
381 Park Avenue South, Suite 1420
New York, NY 10016
(212) 545-7510
http://www.ncld.org

National Center for Post Traumatic Stress Disorder (NCPTSD)
(802) 296-6300
http://www.ncptsd.va.gov/facts/general/fs_what_is_ptsd.html

National Mental Health Association (NMHA)
2000 North Beauregard Street, 6th Floor
Alexandria, VA 22311
(703) 684-7722 or (800) 969-6642
http://www.nmha.org

Online Asperger Syndrome Information and Support (OASIS)
http://www.udel.edu/bkirby/asperger

Wrightslaw
http://www.wrightslaw.com

Resource B

ASCA Position Statement on the Professional School Counselor and Students With Special Needs

Professional school counselors encourage and support all students' academic, personal/social and career development through comprehensive school counseling programs. Professional school counselors are committed to helping all students realize their potential and make adequate yearly progress despite challenges that may result from identified disabilities and other special needs.

NOTE: Adopted 1999; revised 2004

RATIONALE

Professional school counselors have increasingly important roles in working with students who have special needs. State and federal laws require schools to provide an equitable education for all students, including those with special needs. Components of federal laws such as due process, individual educational programs, least restrictive environment, and other plans for students with accommodations and modifications, provide opportunities to use the professional school counselor's skills to benefit students with special needs. Professional school counselors work with students with special needs both in special class settings and in the regular classroom and are a key component in assisting with transitions to postsecondary options. It is particularly important that the professional school counselor's role in these procedures is clearly defined and is in compliance with laws and local policies.

THE PROFESSIONAL SCHOOL COUNSELOR'S ROLE

When appropriate, interventions in which the professional school counselor participates may include but are not limited to:

- leading school counseling activities as a part of the comprehensive school counseling program
- providing collaborative services consistent with those services provided to students through the comprehensive school counseling program
- serving on the school's multidisciplinary team that identifies students who may need assessments to determine special needs within the scope and practice of the professional school counselor
- collaborating with other student support specialists in the delivery of services
- providing group and individual counseling
- advocating for students with special needs in the school and in the community

- assisting with the establishment and implementation of plans for accommodations and modifications
- providing assistance with transitions from grade to grade as well as postsecondary options
- consulting and collaborating with staff and parents to understand the special needs of these students
- making referrals to appropriate specialists within the school system and in the community

The professional school counselor advocates for students with special needs and is one of many school staff members who may be responsible for providing information as written plans are prepared for students with special needs. The professional school counselor has a responsibility to be a part of designing portions of these plans related to the comprehensive school counseling program, but it is inappropriate for the professional school counselor to serve in supervisory or administrative roles such as:

- making decisions regarding placement or retention
- serving in any supervisory capacity related to the implementation of IDEA
- serving as the LEA representative for the team writing the IEP
- coordinating the 504 planning team
- supervising of the implementation of the 504 plan

The professional school counselor continues to seek opportunities for professional development to better understand special needs in regards to assessment, research and legislation. The professional school counselor also collaborates with members of the community who are providing services to students with special needs.

SUMMARY

The professional school counselor takes an active role in providing a comprehensive school counseling program to students with special needs. Professional school counselors advocate for all students and provide collaborative services to students with special needs consistent with those services provided to students through the comprehensive school counseling program.

Resource C

ASCA's Ethical Standards for School Counselors

PREAMBLE

The American School Counselor Association (ASCA) is a professional organization whose members are certified/licensed in school counseling with unique qualifications and skills to address the academic, personal/social and career development needs of all students. Professional school counselors are advocates, leaders, collaborators and consultants who create opportunities for equity in access and success in educational opportunities by connecting their programs to the mission of schools and subscribing to the following tenets of professional responsibility:

- Each person has the right to be respected, be treated with dignity and have access to a comprehensive school counseling program that advocates for and affirms all students from diverse populations regardless of ethnic/racial status, age, economic status, special needs, English as a second

NOTE: ASCA's Ethical Standards for School Counselors were adopted by the ASCA Delegate Assembly, March 19, 1984, and revised March 27, 1992; June 25, 1998; and June 26, 2004. Versions in both English and Spanish are available online at www.schoolcounselor .org.

language or other language group, immigration status, sexual orientation, gender, gender identity/expression, family type, religious/spiritual identity and appearance.

- Each person has the right to receive the information and support needed to move toward self-direction and self-development and affirmation within one's group identities, with special care being given to students who have historically not received adequate educational services: students of color, low socio-economic students, students with disabilities and students with nondominant language backgrounds.
- Each person has the right to understand the full magnitude and meaning of his/her educational choices and how those choices will affect future opportunities.
- Each person has the right to privacy and thereby the right to expect the counselor-student relationship to comply with all laws, policies and ethical standards pertaining to confidentiality in the school setting.

In this document, ASCA specifies the principles of ethical behavior necessary to maintain the high standards of integrity, leadership and professionalism among its members. The Ethical Standards for School Counselors were developed to clarify the nature of ethical responsibilities held in common by school counseling professionals. The purposes of this document are to:

- Serve as a guide for the ethical practices of all professional school counselors regardless of level, area, population served or membership in this professional association;
- Provide self-appraisal and peer evaluations regarding counselor responsibilities to students, parents/guardians, colleagues and professional associates, schools, communities and the counseling profession; and
- Inform those served by the school counselor of acceptable counselor practices and expected professional behavior.

A.1. Responsibilities to Students

The professional school counselor:

a. Has a primary obligation to the student, who is to be treated with respect as a unique individual.

b. Is concerned with the educational, academic, career, personal and social needs and encourages the maximum development of every student.
c. Respects the student's values and beliefs and does not impose the counselor's personal values.
d. Is knowledgeable of laws, regulations and policies relating to students and strives to protect and inform students regarding their rights.

A.2. Confidentiality

The professional school counselor:

a. Informs students of the purposes, goals, techniques and rules of procedure under which they may receive counseling at or before the time when the counseling relationship is entered. Disclosure notice includes the limits of confidentiality such as the possible necessity for consulting with other professionals, privileged communication, and legal or authoritative restraints. The meaning and limits of confidentiality are defined in developmentally appropriate terms to students.
b. Keeps information confidential unless disclosure is required to prevent clear and imminent danger to the student or others or when legal requirements demand that confidential information be revealed. Counselors will consult with appropriate professionals when in doubt as to the validity of an exception.
c. In absence of state legislation expressly forbidding disclosure, considers the ethical responsibility to provide information to an identified third party who, by his/her relationship with the student, is at a high risk of contracting a disease that is commonly known to be communicable and fatal. Disclosure requires satisfaction of all of the following conditions:
   - Student identifies partner or the partner is highly identifiable
   - Counselor recommends the student notify partner and refrain from further high-risk behavior
   - Student refuses
   - Counselor informs the student of the intent to notify the partner
   - Counselor seeks legal consultation as to the legalities of informing the partner

d. Requests of the court that disclosure not be required when the release of confidential information may potentially harm a student or the counseling relationship.

e. Protects the confidentiality of students' records and releases personal data in accordance with prescribed laws and school policies. Student information stored and transmitted electronically is treated with the same care as traditional student records.

f. Protects the confidentiality of information received in the counseling relationship as specified by federal and state laws, written policies and applicable ethical standards. Such information is only to be revealed to others with the informed consent of the student, consistent with the counselor's ethical obligation.

g. Recognizes his/her primary obligation for confidentiality is to the student but balances that obligation with an understanding of the legal and inherent rights of parents/guardians to be the guiding voice in their children's lives.

A.3. Counseling Plans

The professional school counselor:

a. Provides students with a comprehensive school counseling program that includes a strong emphasis on working jointly with all students to develop academic and career goals.

b. Advocates for counseling plans supporting students' right to choose from the wide array of options when they leave secondary education. Such plans will be regularly reviewed to update students regarding critical information they need to make informed decisions.

A.4. Dual Relationships

The professional school counselor:

a. Avoids dual relationships that might impair his/her objectivity and increase the risk of harm to the student (e.g., counseling one's family members, close friends or associates).

If a dual relationship is unavoidable, the counselor is responsible for taking action to eliminate or reduce the potential for harm. Such safeguards might include informed consent, consultation, supervision and documentation.
  b. Avoids dual relationships with school personnel that might infringe on the integrity of the counselor/student relationship.

A.5. Appropriate Referrals

The professional school counselor:

  a. Makes referrals when necessary or appropriate to outside resources. Appropriate referrals may necessitate informing both parents/guardians and students of applicable resources and making proper plans for transitions with minimal interruption of services. Students retain the right to discontinue the counseling relationship at any time.

A.6. Group Work

The professional school counselor:

  a. Screens prospective group members and maintains an awareness of participants' needs and goals in relation to the goals of the group. The counselor takes reasonable precautions to protect members from physical and psychological harm resulting from interaction within the group.
  b. Notifies parents/guardians and staff of group participation if the counselor deems it appropriate and if consistent with school board policy or practice.
  c. Establishes clear expectations in the group setting and clearly states that confidentiality in group counseling cannot be guaranteed. Given the developmental and chronological ages of minors in schools, the counselor recognizes the tenuous nature of confidentiality for minors renders some topics inappropriate for group work in a school setting.
  d. Follows up with group members and documents proceedings as appropriate.

A.7. Danger to Self or Others

The professional school counselor:

a. Informs parents/guardians or appropriate authorities when the student's condition indicates a clear and imminent danger to the student or others. This is to be done after careful deliberation and, where possible, after consultation with other counseling professionals.

b. Will attempt to minimize threats to a student and may choose to (1) inform the student of actions to be taken, (2) involve the student in a three-way communication with parents/guardians when breaching confidentiality or (3) allow the student to have input as to how and to whom the breach will be made.

A.8. Student Records

The professional school counselor:

a. Maintains and secures records necessary for rendering professional services to the student as required by laws, regulations, institutional procedures and confidentiality guidelines.

b. Keeps sole-possession records separate from students' educational records in keeping with state laws.

c. Recognizes the limits of sole-possession records and understands these records are a memory aid for the creator and in absence of privileged communication may be subpoenaed and may become educational records when they (1) are shared with others in verbal or written form, (2) include information other than professional opinion or personal observations and/or (3) are made accessible to others.

d. Establishes a reasonable timeline for purging sole-possession records or case notes. Suggested guidelines include shredding sole possession records when the student transitions to the next level, transfers to another school or graduates. Careful discretion and deliberation should be applied before destroying sole-possession records that may be needed by a court of law such as notes on child abuse, suicide, sexual harassment or violence.

A.9. Evaluation, Assessment, and Interpretation

The professional school counselor:

a. Adheres to all professional standards regarding selecting, administering and interpreting assessment measures and only utilizes assessment measures that are within the scope of practice for school counselors.
b. Seeks specialized training regarding the use of electronically based testing programs in administering, scoring and interpreting that may differ from that required in more traditional assessments.
c. Considers confidentiality issues when utilizing evaluative or assessment instruments and electronically based programs.
d. Provides interpretation of the nature, purposes, results and potential impact of assessment/evaluation measures in language the student(s) can understand.
e. Monitors the use of assessment results and interpretations, and takes reasonable steps to prevent others from misusing the information.
f. Uses caution when utilizing assessment techniques, making evaluations and interpreting the performance of populations not represented in the norm group on which an instrument is standardized.
g. Assesses the effectiveness of his/her program in having an impact on students' academic, career and personal/social development through accountability measures especially examining efforts to close achievement, opportunity and attainment gaps.

A.10. Technology

The professional school counselor:

a. Promotes the benefits of and clarifies the limitations of various appropriate technological applications. The counselor promotes technological applications (1) that are appropriate for the student's individual needs, (2) that the student understands how to use and (3) for which follow-up counseling assistance is provided.

b. Advocates for equal access to technology for all students, especially those historically underserved.

c. Takes appropriate and reasonable measures for maintaining confidentiality of student information and educational records stored or transmitted over electronic media including although not limited to fax, electronic mail and instant messaging.

d. While working with students on a computer or similar technology, takes reasonable and appropriate measures to protect students from objectionable and/or harmful online material.

e. Who is engaged in the delivery of services involving technologies such as the telephone, videoconferencing and the Internet takes responsible steps to protect students and others from harm.

A.11. Student Peer Support Program

The professional school counselor:

Has unique responsibilities when working with student-assistance programs. The school counselor is responsible for the welfare of students participating in peer-to-peer programs under his/her direction.

B. RESPONSIBILITIES TO PARENTS/GUARDIANS

B.1. Parent Rights and Responsibilities

The professional school counselor:

a. Respects the rights and responsibilities of parents/guardians for their children and endeavors to establish, as appropriate, a collaborative relationship with parents/guardians to facilitate the student's maximum development.

b. Adheres to laws, local guidelines and ethical standards of practice when assisting parents/guardians experiencing family difficulties that interfere with the student's effectiveness and welfare.

c. Respects the confidentiality of parents/guardians.

d. Is sensitive to diversity among families and recognizes that all parents/guardians, custodial and noncustodial, are vested with certain rights and responsibilities for the welfare of their children by virtue of their role and according to law.

B.2. Parents/Guardians and Confidentiality

The professional school counselor:

a. Informs parents/guardians of the counselor's role with emphasis on the confidential nature of the counseling relationship between the counselor and student.

b. Recognizes that working with minors in a school setting may require counselors to collaborate with students' parents/guardians.

c. Provides parents/guardians with accurate, comprehensive and relevant information in an objective and caring manner, as is appropriate and consistent with ethical responsibilities to the student.

d. Makes reasonable efforts to honor the wishes of parents/guardians concerning information regarding the student, and in cases of divorce or separation exercises a good-faith effort to keep both parents informed with regard to critical information with the exception of a court order.

C. RESPONSIBILITIES TO COLLEAGUES AND PROFESSIONAL ASSOCIATES

C.1. Professional Relationships

The professional school counselor:

a. Establishes and maintains professional relationships with faculty, staff and administration to facilitate an optimum counseling program.

b. Treats colleagues with professional respect, courtesy and fairness. The qualifications, views and findings of colleagues are represented to accurately reflect the image of competent professionals.

    c. Is aware of and utilizes related professionals, organizations and other resources to whom the student may be referred.

C.2. Sharing Information with Other Professionals

The professional school counselor:

    a. Promotes awareness and adherence to appropriate guidelines regarding confidentiality, the distinction between public and private information and staff consultation.
    b. Provides professional personnel with accurate, objective, concise and meaningful data necessary to adequately evaluate, counsel and assist the student.
    c. If a student is receiving services from another counselor or other mental health professional, the counselor, with student and/or parent/guardian consent, will inform the other professional and develop clear agreements to avoid confusion and conflict for the student.
    d. Is knowledgeable about release of information and parental rights in sharing information.

D. RESPONSIBILITIES TO THE SCHOOL AND COMMUNITY

D.1. Responsibilities to the School

The professional school counselor:

    a. Supports and protects the educational program against any infringement not in students' best interest.
    b. Informs appropriate officials in accordance with school policy of conditions that may be potentially disruptive or damaging to the school's mission, personnel and property while honoring the confidentiality between the student and counselor.
    c. Is knowledgeable and supportive of the school's mission and connects his/her program to the school's mission.
    d. Delineates and promotes the counselor's role and function in meeting the needs of those served. Counselors will

notify appropriate officials of conditions that may limit or curtail their effectiveness in providing programs and services.

e. Accepts employment only for positions for which he/she is qualified by education, training, supervised experience, state and national professional credentials and appropriate professional experience.

f. Advocates that administrators hire only qualified and competent individuals for professional counseling positions.

g. Assists in developing: (1) curricular and environmental conditions appropriate for the school and community, (2) educational procedures and programs to meet students' developmental needs and (3) a systematic evaluation process for comprehensive, developmental, standards-based school counseling programs, services and personnel. The counselor is guided by the findings of the evaluation data in planning programs and services.

D.2. Responsibility to the Community

The professional school counselor:

a. Collaborates with agencies, organizations and individuals in the community in the best interest of students and without regard to personal reward or remuneration.

b. Extends his/her influence and opportunity to deliver a comprehensive school counseling program to all students by collaborating with community resources for student success.

E. RESPONSIBILITIES TO SELF

E.1. Professional Competence

The professional school counselor:

a. Functions within the boundaries of individual professional competence and accepts responsibility for the consequences of his/her actions.

b. Monitors personal well-being and effectiveness and does not participate in any activity that may lead to inadequate professional services or harm to a student.

   c. Strives through personal initiative to maintain professional competence including technological literacy and to keep abreast of professional information. Professional and personal growth are ongoing throughout the counselor's career.

E.2. Diversity

The professional school counselor:

   a. Affirms the diversity of students, staff and families.
   b. Expands and develops awareness of his/her own attitudes and beliefs affecting cultural values and biases and strives to attain cultural competence.
   c. Possesses knowledge and understanding about how oppression, racism, discrimination and stereotyping affects her/him personally and professionally.
   d. Acquires educational, consultation and training experiences to improve awareness, knowledge, skills and effectiveness in working with diverse populations: ethnic/racial status, age, economic status, special needs, ESL or ELL, immigration status, sexual orientation, gender, gender identity/expression, family type, religious/spiritual identity and appearance.

F. RESPONSIBILITIES TO THE PROFESSION

F.1. Professionalism

The professional school counselor:

   a. Accepts the policies and procedures for handling ethical violations as a result of maintaining membership in the American School Counselor Association.
   b. Conducts herself/himself in such a manner as to advance individual ethical practice and the profession.
   c. Conducts appropriate research and reports findings in a manner consistent with acceptable educational and psychological research practices. The counselor advocates for the protection of the individual student's identity when using data for research or program planning.

  d. Adheres to ethical standards of the profession, other official policy statements, such as ASCA's position statements, role statement and the ASCA National Model, and relevant statutes established by federal, state and local governments, and, when these are in conflict, works responsibly for change.
  e. Clearly distinguishes between statements and actions made as a private individual and those made as a representative of the school counseling profession.
  f. Does not use his/her professional position to recruit or gain clients, consultees for his/her private practice or to seek and receive unjustified personal gains, unfair advantage, inappropriate relationships or unearned goods or services.

F.2. Contribution to the Profession

The professional school counselor:

  a. Actively participates in local, state and national associations fostering the development and improvement of school counseling.
  b. Contributes to the development of the profession through the sharing of skills, ideas and expertise with colleagues.
  c. Provides support and mentoring to novice professionals.

G. MAINTENANCE OF STANDARDS

Ethical behavior among professional school counselors, association members and nonmembers, is expected at all times. When there exists serious doubt as to the ethical behavior of colleagues or if counselors are forced to work in situations or abide by policies that do not reflect the standards as outlined in these Ethical Standards for School Counselors, the counselor is obligated to take appropriate action to rectify the condition. The following procedure may serve as a guide:

  1. The counselor should consult confidentially with a professional colleague to discuss the nature of a complaint to see if the professional colleague views the situation as an ethical violation.

2. When feasible, the counselor should directly approach the colleague whose behavior is in question to discuss the complaint and seek resolution.

3. If resolution is not forthcoming at the personal level, the counselor shall utilize the channels established within the school, school district, the state school counseling association and ASCA's Ethics Committee.

4. If the matter still remains unresolved, referral for review and appropriate action should be made to the Ethics Committees in the following sequence:
   - state school counselor association
   - American School Counselor Association

5. The ASCA Ethics Committee is responsible for:
   - educating and consulting with the membership regarding ethical standards
   - periodically reviewing and recommending changes in code
   - receiving and processing questions to clarify the application of such standards; questions must be submitted in writing to the ASCA Ethics chair.
   - handling complaints of alleged violations of the ethical standards. At the national level, complaints should be submitted in writing to the ASCA Ethics Committee, c/o the Executive Director, American School Counselor Association, 1101 King St., Suite 625, Alexandria, VA 22314.

References

American School Counselor Association (ASCA). (2004). *Position statement: Students with special needs.* Alexandria, VA: Author. Retrieved October 10, 2005, from www.schoolcounselor.org.

American School Counselor Association (ASCA). (2005a). *The ASCA national model: A framework for school counseling programs executive summary.* Retrieved October 5, 2005, from www.schoolcounselor.org.

American School Counselor Association (ASCA). (2005b). *Back-to-school tips.* Retrieved from http://www.schoolcounselor.org.

Americans with Disabilities Act of 1990, P.L. 101–336 S.993 (1990). Retrieved October 10, 2005, from http://www.usdoj.gov/crt/ada/.

Association for Children and Adults with Learning Disabilities. (2004). Retrieved October 22, 2005, from http://www.acldonline.org.

Autism Society of Southeastern Wisconsin. *Autism spectrum disorders 2006 resource directory.* Retrieved October 10, 2006, from www.assew.org.

Bangert, A. W., & Baumberger, J. P. (2001). Designing effective prereferral interventions: Key questions the school counselor should know and ask. *Professional Issues in Counseling Online Journal.* Retrieved September 28, 2005, from http://www.shsu.edu/~piic/winter2001/Bangert.htm.

Beck, J. S., Beck, A., & Jolly, J. B. (2001). *Beck Youth Inventory.* The Psychological Corporation.

Becvar, D. S., & Becvar, R. J. (2006, March). *Facilitating resilience in clinical practice.* Paper presented at the Distinguished Lecture Series, South Dakota State University Department of Counseling and Human Resource Development, Sioux Falls, SD.

Beutler, L., & Harwood, T. (2000). *Prescriptive psychotherapy: A practical guide to systematic treatment selection.* New York: Oxford University Press.

Centers for Disease Control and Prevention. (2005, April 6). *How common is autism spectrum disorder (ASDs)?* Retrieved October 24, 2005, from http://www.cdc.gov/ncbddd/autism/asd_common.htm.

Cook, J. B. & Kaffenberger, C. J. (2003). Solution shop: A solution-focused counseling and study skills program for middle school. *Professional School Counseling, 7*(2), 116–123.

Cottone, R. & Tarvydas, V. (2003). *Ethical and professional issues in counseling* (2nd ed.). Upper Saddle, NJ: Merrill Prentice Hall.

Council for Exceptional Children. (2005, Winter). *New flexibility in testing students with disabilities a positive step.* Retrieved January 6, 2006, from http://www.cec.sped.org/bk/cectoday/winter_2005/leadstory_1.html.

Couwenhoven, T. (2001). Sexuality education: Building a foundation for healthy attitudes. *Disabilities Solutions, 4*(5), 1–13.

De Jong, P., & Berg, I. K. (2002). *Interviewing for solutions* (2nd ed.). Pacific Grove, CA: Brooks/Cole.

Education Trust. (n.d.). African American achievement in America. Retrieved January 5, 2006, from http://www2.edtrust.org/NR/rdonlyres/9AB4AC88–7301–43FF-81A3-EB94807B917F/0/AfAmer_Achivement.pdf.

Education Trust. (n.d.). Latino achievement in America. Retrieved January 5, 2006, from http://www2.edtrust.org/NR/rdonlyres/7DC36C7E-EBBE43BB-8392-CDC618E1F762/0/LatAchievEnglish.pdf.

Education Trust (n.d.). Yes we can: Telling truths and dispelling myths about race and education in America. Retrieved October 10, 2006, from http://www2.edtrust.org/EdTrust/Press+Room/Yes+We+Can.htm.

Feld, A. D. (2005). The health insurance portability and accountability act (HIPAA): Its broad effect on practice. *American Journal of Gastroenterology, 100*, 1440–1443.

Fenell, D. L., & Weinhold, B. K. (1997). *Counseling families: An introduction to marriage and family therapy.* Denver, CO: Love.

Fine, M. J. (1991). *Collaboration with parents of exceptional children.* Brandon, VT: Clinical Psychology.

Fisher, R. & Ury, W. (1991). *Getting to yes: Negotiating agreement without giving in.* New York: Houghton Mifflin.

Gargiulo, R. M. (2004). *Young children with special needs.* Clifton Park, NY: Thomson Delmar Learning.

Gargiulo, R. M. (2005). *Special education in contemporary society with Infotrac.* Stamford, CT: Thomson Wadsworth.

Guterman, J. (2006). *Mastering the art of solution-focused counseling.* Alexandria, VA: American Counseling Association.

Halbur, D. A., & Halbur, K. V. (2006). *Developing your theoretical orientation in counseling and psychotherapy.* Boston: Pearson Education.

Harper, L. (2005, August 21). No Child Left Behind's impact on special education. *Online Newshour.* Retrieved January 17, 2006, from http://www.pbs.org/newshour/bb/education/nclb/specialneeds.

Harry, B. (1992). Restructuring the participation of African-American parents in special education. *Exceptional Children, 5,* 123–131.

Hatch, T., & Bowers, J. (2002). *The block to build on.* Retrieved October 15, 2005, from http://www.schoolcounselor.org/files/BuildingBlocks .pdf.

Hubble, M. A., Duncan, B. L., & Miller, S. D. (1999). *The heart and soul of change.* Washington, DC: American Psychological Association.

Individuals with Disabilities Education Act (IDEA). Code of Federal Regulations, Title 34, C.F.R. § 300.532(b), 20 U.S.C. § 1400–1476. (1990, 1995, 1997, 2004).

Kosine, N. (2005, December 16). Effective college transition planning for students with learning disabilities: What does the research tell us? *School Counseling Research Brief, 3*(4).

Learning Disabilities Association. (n.d.). *Transitioning from college to work: LDA fact sheet.* Retrieved October 25, 2005, from http://www .ldanatl.org/aboutld/adults/post_secondary/transitioning.asp

Lockhart, E. J. (1998, June). *The school counselor's role in special education and Section 504.* Paper presented at the meeting of the American School Counselor Association, San Antonio, TX.

Martin, R. (2006). *IEP goals.* Retrieved on November 17, 2005 from http://www.reedmartin.com.

McConaughy, S. (2005). *Assessment to intervention.* New York: Guilford Press.

Metcalf, L. (1998). *Solution focused counseling groups: Ideas for groups in private practice, schools, agencies, and treatment programs.* New York: The Free Press.

Meyer, D. J., & Vadasy, P. F. (1994). *Sibshops: Workshops for siblings of children with special needs.* Baltimore, MD: Brookes Publishing Co.

Mitchell, R. W. (1991). Documentation in counseling records. In T. P. Remley, Jr. (Ed.), *The ACA legal series: Vol. 2.* (pp. 1–71). Alexandria, VA: The American Counseling Association.

National Center for Education Statistics. (2004). *Digest of educational statistics.* Retrieved November 22, 2005, from http://nces.ed.gov/ programs/digest/d04.

National Center for Learning Disabilities (NCLD). (2005). *LD at a glance.* Retrieved October 25, 2005, from http://www.ncld.org.

National Center for Learning Disabilities. (2004). *LD fast facts.* Retrieved October 25, 2005, from http://www.ncld.org/index.php?option= content&task=view&id=483.

National Dissemination Center for Children with Disabilities. (n.d.). *General information: How does IDEA define the 13 disability categories?* Retrieved February 11, 2006, from http://www.nichcy.org/pubs/ genresc/gr3.htm#categories.

No Child Left Behind Act of 2001, 20 USC § 6301 et seq. (2002).

Parent Advocacy Coalition for Educational Rights (PACER). (2004). *Juvenile justice.* Retrieved October 22, 2005, from http://www.pacer.org.

Pipher, M. (1996). *In the shelter of each other: Rebuilding our families.* New York: Ballantine.

Power, T. J., & Bartholomew, K. L. (1987). Family-school relationship patterns: An ecological assessment. *School Psychology Review, 16*(4), 498–512.

Reynolds, C., & Kamphaus, R. (2004a). *BASC portable observation program.* Circle Pines, MN: AGS Publishing.

Reynolds, C., & Kamphaus, R. (2004b). *Behavior assessment system for children.* (2nd ed.). Circle Pines, MN: AGS Publishing.

Roberts, R. L., & Baumberger, J. P. (1999). T.R.E.A.T.: A model for constructing counseling goals and objectives for students with special needs. *Intervention in School and Clinic, 34*(4), 239–243.

Robertson, G. (2006, January 21). Shadow siblings: Children growing up with siblings who have special needs share how those bonds sometimes scar, but more often enrich their lives. *The Minneapolis Star-Tribune,* pp. E1, E4.

Sailor, W., & Roger, B. (2005). Rethinking inclusion: Schoolwide applications. *Phi Delta Kappan, 86*(7), 503–509.

Samuels, C. A. (2005). Special educators discuss NCLB at national meeting. *Education Week, 24*(3), 12.

Sattler, J. M. (1998). *Clinical and forensic interviewing of children and families: Guidelines for the mental health, education, pediatric, and child maltreatment fields.* San Diego, CA: Author.

Seligman, M. (1979). *Strategies for helping parents of exceptional children.* New York: The Free Press.

Simpson, R. L., LaCava, P. G., & Graner, P. S. (2004). The No Child Left Behind Act: Challenges and implications for educators. *Intervention in School and Clinic, 40*(2), 67–75.

Sklare, G. (2004). *A soluction-focusued approach for school counselors and administrators* (2nd ed.). Thousand Oaks, CA: Corwin Press.

Slade, J. C. (1988). Why siblings of handicapped children need the attention and help of the counselor. *The School Counselor, 36,* 107–111.

Sommers-Flanagan, R. & Sommers-Flanagan, J. (2006). *Hope for special-need students and their parents.* Retrieved January 10, 2006, from http://www.schoolcounselor.org.

Taylor, G. (2000). *Parental involvement: A practical guide for collaboration and teamwork for students with disabilities.* Springfield, IL: Charles C Thomas Publisher, Ltd.

Turnbull, A., Turnbull, R., Erwin, E. J., & Soodak, L. C. (2006). *Families, professionals, and exceptionality: Positive outcomes through partnerships and trust* (5th ed.). Upper Saddle River, NJ: Pearson Merrill Prentice Hall.

U.S. Department of Labor. (2005). *Statistics about people with disabilities and employment*. Washington, DC: U.S. Department of Education. [On-line]. Retrieved October 15, 2005, from http://www.dol.gov/odep/pubs/ek01/stats.htm.

U.S. Department of Education. (n.d.). *Family Educational Rights and Privacy Act*. Retrieved October 3, 2005, from http://www.ed.gov/policy/gen/guid/fpco/ferpa/index.hpml.

U.S. Department of Education. (n.d.). *Family compliance office*. Retrieved October 10, 2006, from http://www.ed.gov/policy/gen/guid/fpco/index.html.

U.S. Department of Education. (2005, July 22). *25th Annual Report to congress on implementation of the ADA*. Retrieved January 18, 2006, from http://www.ed.gov/searchResults.jhtml?oq=report+to+congress+ADA.

Vanderbleek, L. M. (2004). Engaging families in school-based mental health treatment. *Journal of Mental Health Counseling, 26*(3), 211–224.

Vocational Rehabilitation Act of 1973, H.R. 8070, P.L. 93–112 Section 504. (1973).

Webb, L. D., & Myrick, R. D. (2003). A group counseling intervention for children with attention deficit disorder. *The School Counselor, 7*, 108–115.

Welfel, E. R. (2002). *Ethics in counseling and psychotherapy: Standards, research and emerging issues* (2nd ed). Pacific Grove, CA: Brooks/Cole.

WikEd. (n.d.) *Sociograms*. Retrieved on November 2, 2005, from http://wik.ed.uiuc.edu/index.php/Sociogram.

Young, M. E. (2005). *Learning the art of helping: Building blocks and techniques* (3rd ed.). Upper Saddle River, NJ: Pearson Education.

Suggested Readings

Alper, S., Schloss, P. J., & Schloss, C. N. (1996). Families of children with disabilities in elementary and middle school: Advocacy models and strategies. *Exceptional Children, 6,* 261–270.

Barkley, R. (1990). *Attention deficit hyperactivity disorder: A handbook for diagnosis and treatment.* New York: Guilford.

Becvar, D. S., & Becvar, R. J. (2006). *Family therapy: A systemic integration* (6th ed.). Boston: Allyn & Bacon.

Bellak, L. (1993). *The Thematic Apperception Test, the Children's Apperception Test, and the Senior Apperception Test in clinical use* (5th ed.). Boston: Allyn & Bacon.

Bragg, R. M., Brown, R. L., & Berninger, V. W. (1992). The impact of congenital and acquired disabilities on the family system: Implications for school counseling. *The School Counselor, 39,* 292–299.

Brame, C. M., Martin, D., & Martin, P. (1998). Counseling the blind or visually impaired child: An examination of behavioral techniques. *Professional School Counseling, 1,* 60–62.

Brigman, G. E., & Campbell, C. (2003). Does implementing a research-based school counseling curriculum enhance student achievement? *Professional School Counseling, 7,* 91–98.

Brigman, G. E., & Campbell, C. (2003). Helping students improve academic achievement and school success behavior. *Professional School Counseling, 7*(2), 91–98.

Buchman, D. (2006). *A special education: One family's journey through the maze of learning disabilities.* Jackson, TN: Perseus Books Group.

Burns, R. C. (1982). *Self-growth in families: Kinetic family drawings (K-F-D) research and applications.* New York: Brunner/Mazel.

Burns, R. C., & Kaufman, S. H. (1970). *Kinetic family drawings (K-F-D): An introduction to understanding children through kinetic drawings.* New York: Brunner/Mazel.

Burns, R. C., & Kaufman, S. H. (1972). *Actions, styles, symbols in kinetic family drawings (K-F-D): An interpretive manual.* New York: Brunner/Mazel.

Carps, A. W., & Carps, M. R. (1997). A systems approach to school counseling. *The School Counselor, 44,* 218–223.

Carter, E., & McGoldrick, M. (1980). *The family life cycle: A framework for family therapy.* New York: Gardner.

Conrad, M. B. (1989). Informing parents that their children may be handicapped. *The School Counselor, 36,* 380–383.

Ellis, A., & Wilde, J. (2002). *Case studies in Rational-Emotive Behavior Therapy with children and adolescents.* Upper Saddle River, NJ: Merrill PrenticeHall.

Filer, P. S. (1983). The school counselor as a parent advocate. *The School Counselor, 30,* 141–145.

Fine, M. J., & Gardner, P. A. (1991). Counseling and education services for families: An empowerment perspective. *Elementary School Guidance and Counseling, 26,* 33–44.

Fowler, M. (1992). *C.H.A.D.D. educators manual.* Plantation, FL: Children & Adults with Attention Deficit Disorder.

Goldstein, S., & Goldstein, M. (1995). *A parent's guide: Attention-deficit hyperactivity disorder in children.* Salt Lake City, UT: The Neurology, Learning, and Behavior Center.

Greer, B. B., Greer, J. G., & Woody, D. E. (1995). The inclusion movement and its impact on counselors. *The School Counselor, 43,* 124, 157.

Grigsby, D. A. (1989). Dialogue: Cross-cultural counseling for exceptional individuals and their families. *National Forum of Special Education Journal, 1,* 67–69.

Hinkle, J. S., & Wells, M. E. (1995). *Family counseling in the schools.* Greensboro, NC: ERIC/CASS.

IDEA 1997: Let's make it work. (1998). Reston, VA: The Council for Exceptional Children.

Lombana, J. H. (1992). Learning disabled students and their families: Implications and strategies for counselors. *Journal of Humanistic Education and Development, 31,* 33–40.

McGinnes, E., & Goldstein, A. P. (1990). *Skillstreaming in early childhood: Teaching prosocial skills to the preschool and kindergarten child.* Champaign, IL: Research Press.

McGinnes, E., Goldstein, A. P., Sprafkin, R. P., & Gershaw, N. J. (1984). *Skillstreaming the elementary school child: A guide for teaching prosocial skills.* Champaign, IL: Research Press.

Millon, T., Millon, C., & Davis, R. (1993). *Millon Adolescent Clinical Inventory (MACI) manual.* Minneapolis, MN: National Computer Systems.

Reston, J. (2006). *Fragile innocence: A father's memoir of his daughter's courageous journey.* New York: Harmony Books.

Silver, L. (1992). *The misunderstood child: A guide for parents of children with learning disabilities.* Bradenton, FL: Human Resources Institute.

Studer, J. R. (2005). *The professional school counselor: An advocate for students.* Knoxville, TN: Thomson Brooks/Cole.

U.S. Department of Education. (1992). *Fourteenth annual report to Congress on the implementation of the Individuals with Disabilities Act.* Washington, DC: Division of Innovation and Development.

U.S. Department of Justice, Civil Rights Division, Coordination and Review Section. (1990). *Americans with Disabilities Act requirements: Fact sheet.* Washington, DC: Author.

Waggoner, K., & Wilgosh, L. (1990). Concerns of families of children with learning disabilities. *Journal of Learning Disabilities, 23,* 97–98, 113.

Walther, T. C., Hazel, J. S., Schumaker, J. B., Vernon, S., & Deshler, D. D. (1991). A program for families with children with learning disabilities. In M. J. Fine (Ed.), *Collaboration with parents of exceptional children* (pp. 219–237). Brandon, VT: Clinical Psychology.

Woody, R. H. (1994). Legislation for children with disabilities: Family therapy under public law 101–476. *American Journal of Family Therapy, 22,* 77–82.

Index

CORWIN
PRESS

The Corwin Press logo—a raven striding across an open book—represents the union of courage and learning. Corwin Press is committed to improving education for all learners by publishing books and other professional development resources for those serving the field of PreK–12 education. By providing practical, hands-on materials, Corwin Press continues to carry out the promise of its motto: **"Helping Educators Do Their Work Better."**

The American School Counselor Association (ASCA) supports school counselors' efforts to help students focus on academic, personal/social, and career development so they achieve success in school and are prepared to lead fulfilling lives as responsible members of society. ASCA provides professional development, advocacy, research, publications and other resources for school counseling professionals around the globe.